Cycles of Life

CYCLES OF LIFE

Bicycling
from Brooklyn to Montreal
in 1968 and 2018

PAUL A. GILJE

STICKY EARTH BOOKS

Also by Paul A. Gilje

To Swear Like a Sailor: Maritime Culture in America, 1750-1850 (2016)

Free Trade and Sailors' Rights in the War of 1812 (2013)

Encyclopedia of Revolutionary America, 3 Volumes, edited, (2010)

*Pirates, Jack Tar, and Memory: New Studies in American Maritime
History in the Age of Sail*, edited with William Pencak (2007)

The Making of the American Republic, 1763-1815 (2006)

*Liberty on the Waterfront: American Maritime Society and Culture
in the Age of Revolution, 1750-1850* (2004)

*Revolution and New Nation (1754-1820), Vol. 3 in The Facts On File
Encyclopedia of American History*, edited, Gary B. Nash, gen. ed. (2003)

Wages of Independence: Capitalism in the Early Republic, edited (1997)

Rioting in America (1996)

American Artisans: Explorations in Social Identity, 1750-1850,
edited with Howard Rock and Robert Asher (1995)

*Keepers of the Revolution: Working Men and Women in New York
During the Early Republic*, edited with Howard Rock (1992)

New York in the Age of the Constitution, edited with William Pencak (1992)

The Road to Mobocracy: Popular Disorder in New York City, 1763 to 1834 (1987)

Copyright © 2019 Paul A. Gilje

Published by
STICKY EARTH BOOKS
⎯⎯꘎⎯⎯
Exton, Pennsylvania
StickyEarth.com

All Rights Reserved

Paperback ISBN 978-0-9986449-3-6
Library of Congress Control Number: 2019939826

DEDICATION

*To Roger, Denis, David, Frances,
and, of course, Ann*

ACKNOWLEDGMENTS

In my history books I have always saved the most personal acknowledgment for last. Given the nature of this book, I will start in reverse order. This book would not exist without my life partner – Ann. As any reader will note, whatever her private thoughts about my proposed ride in 2018, Ann gave me her full support. She encouraged me in my training. During the ride itself, she was always there when I needed her. When I finished drafting this book, she read the entire manuscript, offering her thoughts and suggestions (most of which I followed).

I also must acknowledge the vital role David and Frances Sabatini played in the second ride. The text that follows reveals that David was the perfect riding partner: generous to a fault, he followed my lead and accommodated my every shortfall without a murmur of complaint. Frances was a great travel companion for Ann, was fun to be with in the evenings, and most importantly, allowed David to go on the ride in the first place. Both read the manuscript and offered some suggestions. And, to paraphrase David about my advice to him: I always listened to their advice, and sometimes even followed it.

The ride in 2018 would never have taken place without the ride in 1968. I must therefore thank Denis Boston and Roger Reiersen for joining me in that endeavor. Life is full of twists and turns. All three of us were the closest of friends when I was a teenager not only on the trip to Montreal, but throughout those troubled years. Later, we all moved on and lost touch with one another. I still have not managed to reconnect with Denis. I have, however, maintained contact with Roger since I called him in the spring of 2018. Roger almost joined me on the trip. Unfortunately, he was unable to do so. He has been, however, vicariously with me all the way and has read the manuscript and helped me remember some additional details from 1968.

Other people have also contributed to this book. My daughter, Karin, read the entire manuscript and made several suggestions. Bryan Nies, a graduate student who is finishing his dissertation under my co-direction at the University of Oklahoma, also read the manuscript. Bryan has an incredibly sharp eye and caught a huge faux pas I missed when proof reading. Thanks to Bryan, I was not peddling through up-state New York – as some itinerant salesperson – and instead pedaled my way through the trip.

As I considered different ways of publishing the book, my friend David Kuschner suggested I contact Annette Murray who had helped him publish his own wonderful book on the world view of young children. Thank you David for that suggestion. And thank you Annette for doing such a wonderful job with the cover, the design, and the publishing of *Cycles of Life*.

TABLE OF CONTENTS

Part One

Preparation

Chapter 1

The Idea

NINETEEN SIXTY EIGHT was a horrific year. The Vietnam War raged out of control. The Viet Cong captured Hue and launched an attack on Saigon. American forces retook Hue and beat back the Tet Offensive, although few in the United States considered it a great victory. The weekly body count on the evening news, reinforced by the nightmarish images of the conflict in southeast Asia, left a sinking feeling in the stomachs of even those who supported the war. The rest of the world seemed to be faring little better. The Middle East remained a powder keg after Israel vanquished its Arab foes in the Six Day War the previous year. During the summer of 1968 the Russians invaded Czechoslovakia because the leaders in Prague mistakenly thought they could remain committed to the communist ideal and allow personal freedoms. Several insurgencies and civil wars were being fought across the globe, the most tragic of which was the Biafran Succession movement in southeast Nigeria which led to the starvation and death of as many as a million civilians. As disturbing as these events may have been, Americans remained focused on their own problems. James Earl Ray assassinated Martin Luther King, Jr, on April 4, and black neighborhoods across the nation erupted into rioting. At the Mexico City Olympics in October, African American athletes raised their fists during the national anthem to protest racial injustice. A radicalizing women's movement decried the Miss Ameri-

ca pageant and sought to legalize abortion. Disheartened by
the Vietnam War, President Lyndon Johnson declared that
he would not run for re-election. A three way race emerged
to replace him on the Democratic ticket. Robert F. Kennedy
appeared as the great hope for many in America, only to fall
to an assassin's bullet on June 5. That left the Democratic
nomination contest to the anti-war Eugene McCarthy and
Vice President Hubert Humphrey. In a contentious convention, with police and demonstrators clashing on the streets
of Chicago, the Democratic Party opted for the mainstream
Humphrey. Throughout the year, campuses erupted into protest, as young people across the nation expressed disenchant-
ment with the regular political system. Although the year
ended on a high note with Americans circling the moon,
the nation faced the prospect of Republican Richard Nixon
as president. With all of these momentous events swirling
about, three seventeen-year-olds, almost oblivious to what
was happening in the world, pedaled their way up the Hudson Valley into northern New York, and made their way to
Canada just as they were beginning their senior year in high
school.

The news is almost as dismal fifty years later. In 2018 the
United States is again at war and has soldiers spread from
West Africa to the Middle East and beyond. These wars are
nearly invisible to most Americans – except for those who
are deployed and their families. There are no nightly casualty
reports. Multiple civil wars, across Africa, in Yemen, in Syria,
and elsewhere continue to rage. Starvation and disease beset
several nations in the midst of conflict. Within the United
States, even as many Americans fear an influx of immigrants,
domestic terrorism has emerged as a constant threat. During
the year there were over 300 mass murders – where a lone
and crazed individual "shoots up" a school, a church, or a
shopping center. Politics remains fractious and politicians do
little to curb the availability of guns or to aid the mental-

ly disturbed. Democrats bemoan an imbecile in the White House who seems incapable of telling the truth. Republicans, whatever they might think privately, align themselves with President Trump, playing to a sexist and racist base. For many Trump supporters, the Donald is a tough negotiator who calls it as he sees it and will somehow make America great again. He has also pledged to select Supreme Court justices who oppose abortion. In the middle of the me-too movement, while the nation debated a supreme court appointment that could decide the future of Roe vs Wade and abortion rights, as African Americans declared that black lives matter and athletes knelt to demonstrate their support for equal rights, two old men followed in the path of those teenagers fifty years ago.

At the end of the summer in 1968 I biked from Brooklyn to Montreal; I determined to repeat this journey at the end of the summer of 2018. This book is the story of those two rides and the two years in which they took place. My intention here is to write a travel story about the rides, something of a memoir, and a history that compares the world in 1968 and 2018. As a part of the baby boomer generation, I am one of millions of Americans who are putting aside their workaday world for a life of "leisure." This transition – this twist to the cycles of life – is not easy. In repeating my ride of fifty years ago I sought a physical challenge that I know my generation understands. John F. Kennedy created a physical fitness movement for us when we were children and as adults many of us have embraced a host of activities such as jogging, biking, skiing, tennis, and swimming. Even those of us who have allowed our middles and bottoms to expand too much, know that we should be eating better and be more active. Every time I told someone my age of my planned 2018 ride, she or he immediately agreed it was a great idea. Whether capable or not, they also wished they could go with me. If the physical aspects of the ride were important, so too, were the men-

tal aspects. Yes, the road tour to Montreal allowed me one
last (well maybe not last) physical hurrah. One more time to
prove myself. But this second trek to Canada was more than
a rite of passage and personal challenge. It was an opportunity to apply my professional training as a historian not only to
trace the experience of the two rides, but to underscore some
of the great and not so great transformations brought by the
last half century. History, as I told generations of students, is
the story of change and continuity over time. The ride provided me with an opportunity to examine my own life to
see what had changed in the last fifty years and what had
remained the same. History is also about understanding the
past on its own terms. Too often we look at the past and read
our present into it. Of course there are always similarities –
the continuities – but we must understand that life is funda-
mentally different in every age in the past, including the past
that we have lived through. Despite the litany of bad news in
each year, there are basic differences between 1968 and 2018
that affect everyone. In 1968, there was a sense of division in
the nation between generations, over lifestyle, and over the
war, that threatened revolution. Political divisions run deep
in 2018 between Democrats and Republicans, but no one
expects a revolution. Whatever Donald Trump's daily antics,
whatever tragedies loom on the horizon, they do not match
the horror in 1968 when 300,000 young men faced the draft
and nearly 15,000 died in a war that seemed meaningless to
so many. A comparison between 1968 and 2018 also demon-
strates the interaction between larger developments, ranging
from politics to social norms, and personal experience. This
contrast between the individual and the general has under-
written much of my work as a historian and plays a major
role in this book. In short, by writing about my two great
bicycling adventures I can explore two universes: that of a
seventeen-year-old in 1968 to that of a sixty-seven-year-old
in 2018.

Let's face it, whether in 1968 or 2018, these bicycle rides were a great idea. Great ideas, however, are not always so great when you actually put them into motion – as I remembered from 1968. On my first trip, every time things went a little awry, and they did so almost every day, I remember asking Roger and Denis, my two riding partners in 1968, "Whose idea was this anyway?" I meant the question both rhetorically and ironically, although at age seventeen I did not know what those words meant. I never got an answer. As it turns out, the three of us came up with the idea together. In 2018, on the other hand, the idea was all mine. Something I feared I would have to live with. When things went wrong on the second ride, and they did so almost every day, I knew who to blame – me.

* * *

Roger, Dennis and I were great friends in high school. I had met Denis in the seventh grade and we remained close until he went off to college. Since he attended Cornell and I stayed in Brooklyn, we did not see much of each other thereafter. Roger and I started to pal around together when we were sophomores in high school. Finding ourselves in several classes together, and having a shared lunch hour, we spent more and more time together. I was a bit of a clown back then and a bit of a goof-off. Although more serious, Roger was always willing to joke around outside of the classroom. I did not draw such fine distinctions. We developed our own version of the stand-up Smothers Brothers' routine, without the music. The Smothers Brothers were a folk singing duo and comedy act who had their own television show in the 1960s. In 1968 the Smothers Brothers were at the height of their popularity. They spiced up their act with biting liberal political commentary that became so controversial in those intense years, that in 1969 CBS cancelled their television show because of its left wing political content. Both Roger and I thought the Smothers Brothers were terrific so we developed a series of routines for our friends where Roger played the straight man, Dick, and I was the stuttering farcical Tommy. Denis was not part of the act.

All three of us were smart. Denis was the smartest, but was also the bigger slacker in school. Roger was next in sheer brain power. He was a star in the classroom and graduated high school at the top of the class, at least among the boys (we said boys in those days). He was voted most likely to succeed. Both Denis and Roger went to Cornell. But Roger attended the private part of that Ivy League institution and did so on scholarship. Denis had a mix of okay grades, and tested well over 100 points higher than me on the SAT. He matriculated in Cornell's agricultural school which was cheaper since students paid the same tuition as those in a state college, and was easier to get in. No one at Cornell seemed to wonder what a Brooklyn boy was doing in an AG school. Denis was voted school photographer. My high school grades were a few points higher than Denis's, although not nearly as high as Roger's. I went to Brooklyn College after high school because it accepted me and it was free. I wasn't voted anything in our senior year.

All three of us loved to bike, an unusual activity for teenagers in the late sixties. It was this shared passion that spawned the "idea." We began to talk about doing some sort of long distance bike trip and settled on Montreal since it was doable, only 400 miles, and it would be traveling to a foreign country, a notion that played to our teenage imaginations. The idea of biking to a place where people actually spoke a different language sounded exotic to us. Biking to Cleveland, Ohio, or Richmond, Virginia, places of almost equal distance, just did not cut it.

We were also interested in seeing the Montreal "Expo," a world's fair. As Wikipedia will tell you, the defunct Montreal major league baseball team, which began in 1969, took its name from this event fifty years ago. All three of us had gone to the New York World's Fair in 1964 and 1965 multiple times, but not necessarily together. As born-and-bred New Yorkers, we assumed the Expo would not measure up to our city's fair, but we liked the idea of going anyway. Denis and I went together to the last day of the New York World's Fair on October 25, 1965. We skipped the admission fee by clamoring over a fence near the Belgian exhibition, a recreated village that featured tiled buildings, cobble stones, costumed interpreters and, of course, waffles. For spending money we visited some of the other exhibits that had fountains, we lingered at the back of the crowd, and then, when no one was looking, we scooped up handfuls of coins from the pools. There were no surveillance cameras. Since it was the last day, many of the pavilions had private parties. We slipped into some of these to get free food. As far as the celebrants were concerned, we were just someone's kids. Denis also stole some unfinished mixed drinks left by the celebrants. I can still see him creep along behind a solid white fence and reach his long skinny arm to the top of the waist high barrier and grab a drink. A moment later the hand would reappear and place the empty glass back to its original location.

We did not have a clear idea of what was in store for us either in upstate New York, or in Canada. We knew there would be hills and we had a vague notion of witnessing a bucolic (again, not a word I would use in 1968) landscape. But our experience with the region was minimal. When I was eight, I had spent two weeks visiting an aunt and uncle who were temporarily living in Swanton, Vermont. My uncle's job had dispatched him there to work on the silos that were to be part of the missile defense system then being built. I had vague memories of a New England village with a town square, a pond, and swans. I also remembered a railway covered bridge just west of town that my older brother (who was all of ten) and I walked across. My only other venture north of the Bronx Zoo was to a boy scout camp in Putnam

County, about sixty miles above the city. Studying our road maps, we decided that the west side of the Hudson was hillier, so we determined to bike up the east side. Neither Denis nor Roger had much experience in the region as well.

In high school the three of us had sought out all kinds of urban adventures. Being that we thought of ourselves as Brooklyn street-wise city kids, we never gave a thought to taking the subway to Manhattan. We sometimes traveled to Greenwich Village in the early evening, about a fifty minute ride on the local subway, just to walk the streets. We didn't have the money or the inclination to enter many coffee houses. But we enjoyed the street crowds. I once bumped into Jose Feliciano. I did not know who he was at the time, nor that he was a blind singer. Unfortunately, I shouted at him to watch where he was going. Denis quickly informed me of the visual impairment of the target of my ire. The three of us also ventured to the Apollo Theater in Harlem to see Ray Charles (yes, another blind singer). We wanted to sit in the back to be inconspicuous in what was an otherwise totally African American crowd. The usher insisted on our sitting in the front row to keep us safe and in his sight. That was fine with us, except one of the earlier acts, a ventriloquist, noticed us and had his African American wooden partner make several hilarious comments at our expense. In fact, the "dummy" asked us what we were doing there. We sat there politely, unsure of how to respond. Two of us were Lutheran and had always been taught not to be too overt. As three blond boys from Brooklyn, we knew we stood out in that crowd. We grimaced our way through that experience and made it safely home that day (we went to a matinee intentionally). The Montreal trip would be just another adventure, only beyond the confines of our home town.

* * *

If the 1968 decision was shared and an outgrowth of our rambles through New York City, the 2018 trip was all my idea, hatched on the dusty plains of Oklahoma. I came up with the idea as early as 2016 as I contemplated my oncoming retirement. By then I planned to leave off work in August 2019. There was symmetry in my plan. I had taken the 1968 ride at the beginning of my senior year of high school, on the cusp of a whole new world of adulthood. I would travel to Montreal at the beginning of my last year as a college professor, on the cusp of a whole new world of whatever came after adulthood. I would take the trip the same week of the year. A lot happened in 1968 the week before Labor Day. Not only did three boys from Brooklyn pedal their way to Montreal, but also that was the week the Democrats met in convention in Chicago. Demonstrations by the far left led to violent street confrontations between the Chicago police and the anti-war crowds. In the end, the Democrats selected Humphrey, a left-leaning politician who was too mainstream for the radicals. The Republicans in the meantime went with a paranoid conservative who made all kinds of promises – Richard Milhous Nixon. Waiting in the wings was a Southern populist, George Wallace, who had abandoned the Democratic Party to spout racist nonsense that even appealed to Northern workers who feared the demise of the factory in the region we now know as the rust belt. Fifty years later the nation appeared mired in similar politics. In 2016 the Democrats had a left-leaning mainstream candidate who lost to a man who was Nixon and Wallace rolled into one. Yes, absolutely, I had to do the trip in the same week of the year. Symmetry demanded it.

The fact that I would have to play hooky to do so, only made the timing all the more attractive. In 1968 New York City Public Schools began after Labor Day. In 2018 the University of Oklahoma would start classes in late August. I figured that as a senior tenured professor about to retire, there was not much the university could do about my skipping town for a week. As I told my department chair, "what

are you going to do, fire me?" He laughed, and said it was fine
with him that I took the week off. The dean and the provost
had the same reaction.

There really is no career better than being an academic
– that is if you are willing to suspend life while attending
graduate school for five or six years, manage to get a job, and
go through the ordeal of tenure. Once past that threshold,
ordinarily when you are nearing forty, and accepting the fact
that you will never make oodles of money (at least as a history professor), it is a great life. You get to teach wave after
wave of students. I have even taught the children of students
I had taught years before. I was particularly lucky since I
taught at a research university and I had plenty of time to
read, research, and write (the three "Rs" of a history professor). I therefore spent most of my working hours hidden in
libraries pursuing the lives of dead people. The only down-
side was committee work and listening to the complaints of
some of my less content colleagues whose egos never quite
matched their resumes. As much as some of my colleagues
whined about all of the time they put into their teaching and
how they spent countless hours doing service to the university, I knew our jobs were not like real work. We did not have
to stand on our feet all day by some machine and come home
reeking of oil, as my father had.

As easy as it would have been for me to play hooky that
week, I decided to give up some of the symmetry and retire
before the bike trip to Montreal. I took my last sabbatical in
the spring of 2015. I enjoyed myself too much. Ann and I
had already bought the condo in Philadelphia. On weekdays
I went to the Library Company reading old books published
in the year 1800 for my next research project. I also attended lectures and seminars at the University of Pennsylvania.
Most important, I spent plenty of time as "Pop-Pop" to my
granddaughter. I decided I could get used to this kind of life
and accelerated my plans to retire, aiming for August 2018,

right as I was about to take the big ride. Instead of entering my last year of teaching, I would already be finished with the classroom. There was still some symmetry.

Then plans changed again. The University of Oklahoma offered an early retirement incentive of three quarters of my annual salary. Well, I could be employed in the spring of 2018 and get paid half my salary, or retire and get paid three quarters of my salary. You do not need higher math to understand which would be more money. Of course I would give up some retirement income in the long run – but who cared. I would also be free of all work obligations and living off a pension and social security.

As much as I enjoyed teaching, I understood that the distance between the students and this aging professor was ever expanding. When I began my career as an assistant professor in 1980, I was twenty-nine and only a decade older than most of my students. Although I did not realize it then, my idea that I could be a "friend" to the students was a non-starter. My PhD and professional status had already created a huge opening between me and my students. Ever since then, the yawning chasm between professor and student had only widened. Electronics, especially the iPhone and its clones, had extended that chasm even further. Students felt it was their right to have their devices handy at all times. I insisted on an electronics free classroom. Maintaining that policy was a daily struggle. I chided one student on the second day of classes for looking at her phone, contrary to the stated policy. The next class, there she was in the back of the room punching buttons, and pushing mine, using a handheld device. I sternly reminded her again of my policy. She beamed, "oh Professor, this isn't a phone, it's my calculator!" I told her that my policy banned all electronics and a calculator was an electronic device. I didn't even bother to ask her why she was working with a calculator in a history class. She put the calculator away in a harrumph and quickly dropped the class.

Students complained that I needed to get "with the times" and that I needed to adept my teaching methods to the "individual needs of each student" – this in a lecture hall of 250. They might have even called me a Luddite – if they knew that a Luddite was a machine breaking weaver from early nineteenth-century England. Inspired by the mythical Ned Ludd, and without breaking any machines, I fought the good fight right through my last semester. I began each lecture in that massive American History Survey the same way. I would remind the students that "It was time to put away your devices," and then have the entire class respond "and be left to our own devices." Some of them actually got the message. Regardless, after thirty-eight years of teaching, I was ready to retire.

Transitions are seldom sudden in life. They grow on you. Retirement is like that. I had first thought I would never retire. I loved my job and I had all the intellectual freedom I could want. Plus I had plenty of time to devote to my research. There were days I would just go to the library and not even walk through the department office. No clocks to punch. No one looking over my shoulder. All I had to do was show up a few hours a week to teach. The rest of the time was mine. Of course, you were judged on your research output. That was never a problem for me. Why would I want to leave a job like that? Then, I set age seventy as the magic date. I would get the maximum social security and no hobbling around campus with a walker for me. Then I moved the retirement date to sixty-eight. Okay, I would get a little less social security and pension, but I would also be collecting it for two more years. Then I changed the target to sixty-seven. Finally, I took the plunge at sixty-six.

Even before I gave my final lecture – and it was a bang-up lecture – I knew that the time had come. Somehow I had moved from being the Young Turk with all sorts of new ideas for running things, to an Old Fart, who was all too willing to pontificate on what the next generation should do. When I first came to the University of Oklahoma one of my older colleagues introduced himself as the department's "Nestor." I, along with others in my age cohort, chuckled to ourselves about this self-proclaimed avuncular advisor. We knew from the current leadership that they did not take this old guy seriously since he was out of touch with the fast changing world of 1980. The man had been chairman of the department and even served a stint as dean of the college. He had carried the torch and was now sidelined. In my last few years at Oklahoma I thought about that Nestor many times as I all too willingly shared my wisdom accumulated from decades of experience. Time to go if I had become a Nestor, self-proclaimed or not. Aware of this vanity, I vowed to try not to dictate the future of the department at our meetings. I went to one meeting in my last semester where I stifled myself by biting my tongue so hard that it began to bleed. I did not say a word. I also never attended another department meeting. Time to go, indeed.

Retiring, however, can be scary. What does one do? I recently called one friend who had retired and asked him what he did with his time. He said that he and his wife binge-watched a lot of TV. Ouch. I did not want to go there. Of course, I had one benefit by being a historian. I could still practice the three "Rs" – reading, research, and writing – of history. Thinking ahead, I began working on my next history book, completing a draft of two chapters before handing in my office keys. But I also wanted to do more. I wanted to demonstrate that I still was mentally and physically active.

The bike ride would be my salvation. It would mark the transition to the new life. No doubt, in the recesses of my mind, the trip would also be a way to prove myself. To show that even though I had grown old and that what remained of my hair was white, I could still challenge myself physically.

That physical challenge was important. I had never been an athlete, but had always been athletic. I swam. I ran. I even biked a little. I knew my body had peaked decades ago. Now, I could feel the strength ebb from me. My bones creaked. My back tweaked. I had to get up in the middle of the night to pee. Everyday some new body part hurt. I was not as trim as I would like. Tasks that had once been easy had become a strain.

Chapter 2

Getting Started

I MEANT TO start training during the week before Labor Day in 2017. That would give my aging body a year to get ready for the big trek. That did not happen. Oh, I did take two or three rides of about ten miles with the idea of getting started. But, all in all, I just kept in the same ruts. Running three or four times a week (if you call an eleven minute mile running), teaching my one course, and zipping back and forth on a bike from campus to my home a mile away.

I set a new goal for myself. I would begin training on the first of January. You can ride in Oklahoma most days in the winter, when the highs hover around the 40s and 50s. The weather cooperated, but nothing else did. So getting started did not happen again. We remained in Philadelphia all of January because Ann's mom had broken her leg and was convalescing in our condo. Besides, I injured my own leg somehow, pulling a muscle in my butt. It took weeks to heal. I did not even get any running in. Then, by mid January, I slowly worked myself back into running shape (getting DOWN to the eleven minute mile). Occasionally, since I was running inside on a tread mill, I looked askance at the stationary bikes. I found excuses not to hop on one. They were in use. They were about to be in use. Or they were just used. After all, my two miles on the tread mill was enough exercise for one day. And, I would rather just run and not re-injure my butt (the leg injury was really a butt muscle pull – it was even painful to sit on the toilet and wiping myself was torture). So I delayed getting started.

We returned to Oklahoma on February third, just in time to watch the Eagles the next day beat the Patriots in the Super Bowl. Having spent the last two months in Philadelphia, and having watched nearly every building turn green, having watched nearly everyone in the city don green apparel, dog masks, and Eagle paraphernalia, and having bought an Eagles T-Shirt of my own, I was ready to get started. Underdogs – and I must be one myself – ruled. Life again intruded. Yes, I was retired. A man of leisure. A man who had time on his hands. A man who could do whatever he liked. And I was busier than ever. First I had to move out of my office. I emptied four filing cabinets and reviewed my career. I counted the students I taught (over 6,000), the number of reviews I wrote (over 80), tenure cases I evaluated (at least 50), articles and books I refereed (at least 100 articles and over 30 books), hundreds of letters of recommendation (some of which were for students I could not remember), and endless memos and records of committee work. Then there were the fellowship and job applications, along with the inevitable rejection letters. I filled two, yes two, huge recycling containers. I had about four thousand books. I gave three thousand away. Worse, as I packed a thousand books into thirty four boxes, I injured my right shoulder. When I rode my bike to the office (I almost said work, but technically I was retired and had no work), the pain shot down my arm. At home, Ann and I readied the house for sale. We moved furniture, de-cluttered, cleaned everything. At the end of the month we signed a contract with our real estate agent. Two days later the house had been sold. Now, we had to prepare to move in earnest. Getting started was not happening soon. In March we packed and packed and packed. We also sold, donated, or threw away about two thirds of our possessions as we were heading across the country and downsizing from a 2400 square foot house to a 1400 square foot condo that was already furnished. And my arm still ached. I had also decided to give myself a belated retirement party so we had to make those arrangements as well. In short, I had neither time nor energy to spare in March or April. Getting started was not happening again. We closed the sale of our house on the morning of April 26 and set out for Philadelphia that afternoon – I will spare the reader the panicked last minute packing – arriving on April 28, just in time for my granddaughter's fifth birthday party the next day! By then, everything ached – not just my arm. Maybe I would never get started.

* * *

While we were preoccupied with our own little world, Ann and I were aghast at the procession of news stories coming out of Washington. As seniors, we watch way too much television news and read way too much print media. The result was a state of dudgeon over the daily parade of stories revolving around Donald Trump. Trump promised to run the government like a business. He has kept his word. As a businessman Trump was all bravado and bullying, often ignoring the law whenever his interests and ego dictated. He has run the White House the same way – out of his hip pocket. In 1968 many Americans began to doubt the wisdom and veracity of those in government. Pronouncements from the president and his generals that the Vietnam War was almost won did not make much sense in the face of the constant litany of images seen on TV and in the face of the Tet Offensive. Johnson and company were at least trying to grapple with reality. When Johnson learned that Walter Cronkite's investigation into the war suggested that the conflict was unwinnable, the president reportedly declared "If I've lost Cronkite, I've lost Middle America." Today, Trump's method of defusing evidence of his untruths is to lambast the media (except Fox News) and decry its use of "fake news."

It is almost as if Trump does not care what the story is, all he wants is to make sure that he is the headline. I suspect that he believes he can bury yesterday's outrage with today's outrage and that the succession of absurdities will leave both his supporters and his opponents numb. In January Trump asked his cabinet why so many immigrants came from "s–thole countries" and then wondered out loud why we did not get more immigrants from countries like Norway, unaware that when immigrants did come from places like Norway – or the Germany of his own Drumpf family – those countries were s–tholes themselves. In response to the Parkland school shooting in February, Trump suggested that teachers carry guns in schools, even though most teachers opposed the idea. In March, Trump removed some of the adults from his cabinet, leaving many Americans worried what an unrestrained Trump might do on the world stage – he promptly accepted an invitation to meet with Kim Jong-un, the North Korean dictator who Trump had called "little rocket man" and who he now raised to the status of statesman on par with the president of the United States. The following month the FBI raided the home of Michael Cohen, Trump's "fixer" lawyer, who had arranged hush money payments to stripper Stormy Daniels for an alleged affair with Trump. With headlines like these, being preoccupied with moving from Oklahoma and getting ready for my bike ride sounded better and better.

* * *

I was planning to begin training on May 1. But that did not happen. Life intruded. I painted the trim on the study's baseboard instead. I was expecting the delivery of the 34 boxes of books and thought it best to have everything painted before they arrived. I was finished by early afternoon and could have started then. I took a nap instead.

On May 2, at 6:34 PM I finally got started. The temperature, after a cold spring, hovered near ninety and everyone headed out of doors. I hopped on my bike and wormed my way along the Schuylkill River Trail through crowds of strollers (both those idly walking and the vehicles that carry young children), dog walkers, runners, skate boarders, and an assortment of humanity. I would add that I had to pass other bike riders as well. Except, given my speed and timidity in the urban crowd, they passed me. The good news was that there was plenty to look at. There were scads of interesting people, especially young women wearing spandex and running bras. I made it to the Falls Bridge and back, a twelve mile circuit. I was on my bike the next morning and repeated the trip. Wow, twenty four miles in two days. Of course I napped both days, and took the third day off. But I was on my way.

* * *

Over the next weeks I got to know that trail well. Rivers have a certain false timelessness about them. Watching the stream glide along, it is easy to imagine the decades and even centuries gently passing by. This is a false impression. Rivers are constantly changing, either through nature or by the hand of man. The Schuylkill is a different stream now than when George Washington was president and living in Philadelphia, and that Schuylkill was different from the one fished by the Lenape before William Penn established the city of brotherly love. All along the trail are the reminders of a different river. Beginning at the South Street Bridge and as you wend your way along the section built on a boardwalk over the water, you can see the remnants of old wharves along the river's edge. Hemmed in by a highway on one side jammed with traffic, and an embankment supporting an active railway on the other side, the river is a tidal stream here that varies up to six feet during the day. Soon enough you leave the causeway and enter a park squeezed between the rail line and the river. Along the way are a series of bridges that give the river almost a European look. This entire section stands as a testament to the malleability of the river: the rail lines date back to the nineteenth century; the first iterations of the highway were built in the 1920s; and the parks and paths are products of the twenty-first century. After these two miles you reach the Philadelphia Art Museum. The Rocky Steps are on the other side of this neo-classical behemoth. On the river side is the remnant of the old Fairmont Water Works, designed in 1812 and built in stages over the next fifty years. This project was to provide an expanding city with drinkable water taken from the river. Here, too, is the dam that divides the tidal stream from the placid lake-like river that supports Philadelphia's crew regatta schedule. Most of the rowing occurs up river from Boat House Row where you are guaranteed to catch a Thomas Eakins moment: some rower in a racing shell passing under a stone bridge. In fact, I have had multiple such moments, since I was determined to pedal along the trail four or five times a week.

* * *

I did well enough in meeting this goal for a week and a half. Then on a crystal clear mid-week morning I stretched my distance from 12 to 20 miles, riding past the Falls Bridge and on to the outer edge of the city. Ann and I had gone this far before. After riding for less than a mile on the street, you enter Manayunk, an old mill town that is within city limits. Like many of Philadelphia's nineteenth-century working-class districts, Manayunk is undergoing a revival. Young people are moving in. Amid old factory buildings made of stone, rise new condominiums and apartment houses. The main street is crowded with craft beer pubs and boutique shops. Once in this district, you can cut back toward the river and ride along a canal path, which is another remnant of the nineteenth century when the industrial revolution was booming and the canal delivered coal to an energy-hungry nation eager to manufacture. When I was in graduate school in the 1970s, a book called *The Mills of Manayunk* was a must read for anyone interested in this industrializing process. Besides the building conversions and new construction, there are a few old ruins to remind us of those smoke belching days. Instead of a hotbed of industrialization, the current towpath is a serene break from the urban landscape, surrounded by trees and greenery. The biggest hazards here are the geese who might launch an attack at any passerby who wanders too close to their goslings. As the reader can tell, I love this part of the trail, even if its compressed earth surface and its stretches of wooden boardwalk force the rider to slow down.

Having made it to my turnaround point without any incident other than waiting for a pair of geese to guide their brood across the trail, I headed back toward South Street, ten miles away. At mile sixteen of the trip, I felt the rear of my bike, which was always a bit squishy because of the shock absorbers, get even more squishy. Could this be a loss of air in the tire? The answer, unfortunately, was yes. I was not too upset. I viewed my flat tire not as a mishap. Rather it was an opportunity. Flats happen – although back in 1968 we did not have single flat tire on our way to Montreal. I had changed and mended plenty of flat tires in my day. Only I had not done so lately. Well, not in decades. When I had the occasional flat tire as a commuter on my bike, I would simply pop off the tire and take it to a local bike shop. For a few dollars I would let someone else fix my flat. If I got stuck somewhere in Norman, I could always call Ann to the rescue. On this particular day, I was on my own. Ann was out of town visiting our daughter and my son was on a business trip. Great. I can do this. I walked the bike to a nice shady spot since the temperature was rising through the 70s. I took the wheel off. No mean task since this was the rear wheel and I got my hands full of grease from the gear shift sprockets and chain. I found a supersized staple sticking into the sidewall. That would help me to find the hole in the tube, I thought. But I couldn't find that hole. I marked the spot with the piece of chalk in my repair kit and I searched and searched. I pumped the tube with air – yes I even had a hand pump with me. Still, I could not find the leak. Maybe, I thought the problem was elsewhere. I should have been more bold. I should have just patched the spot where I thought the hole would be. Then I could have pumped up the tire and, if I had guessed right, ridden back and bought a replacement inner tube at the local bike shop. The heat must have been getting to me. I was running out of water and I had to pee. It was only a mile to the nearest restroom and maybe four miles from home. I walked the bike back. It killed more than an hour and as it got warmer and warmer I started to get dehydrated. I made it to the bike shop and the young man behind the counter replaced the inner tube and checked the rest of the tire in just a few minutes. I didn't tell him how far I had walked, but I did tell him that I couldn't find the hole in the inner tube. I felt like a rank amateur. I also bought a spare inner tube for the next flat and rode thankfully and sheepishly back to the condo, vowing to be better prepared next time. I showered, called Ann, and took a nap.

Chapter 3

Training

IT WAS ALL so much easier in 1968. Of course I was only seventeen – not sixty-seven. I probably did not have to do anything to get started. I did a great deal of biking back then. Although it would have saved some time, I never took my bike to my high school. This was Brooklyn, after all. No one rode their bikes to school. Or, if they did, they would not have the opportunity of riding it back home since no chain could have prevented it from being stolen or damaged. All through early spring, I walked the mile from school to my home, took out my bike and pedaled as fast as I could through the streets of my old neighborhood down to the water's edge along Shore Road. There was a bike and walking path that hugged the edge of the bay. I sped from the 69th Street Pier to Nellie Bly (near Coney Island) as fast as my athletic legs could take me. Almost no one was there that spring. The weather was not yet warm enough to bring out many people. Back in 1968, even in the summertime, the shore – as we called it – was never too crowded. Today it is often packed with an even greater assortment of humanity than along the Schuylkill: with Hispanics, Blacks, Asians, Hasidic Jews, and burka covered Muslims, as well as some young women in spandex and running bras.

Like the Schuylkill, there is an apparent timelessness to "the shore" in Brooklyn. This, too, is misleading. The walk/bikeway was built on landfill – much of the dirt was dug

out for the Fourth Avenue subway line in the early twentieth century. What was once a wetland, and then a cozy little
cove, is covered with ballfields and parkland. The ridge that
gives my old neighborhood its distinctive name – Bay Ridge
– is still there. Created during the last ice age when melting
snow and ice molded the moraine that shaped Long Island,
it protects my old neighborhood from the storm surges that
have devastated other areas of the city along the oceanfront.
The shore walkway itself has been vulnerable despite a sea-
wall and a protective screen of heavy stones. Over the years
sections of the path have been reclaimed by the sea, only to be
rebuilt and insulated from storm surges by even more stones.
Since my earliest childhood I have always been drawn to
this particular stretch of shoreline where Brooklyn meets the
body of water called the Narrows, the mile-wide straight between the Upper and Lower New York Bays. My high school
faced the Narrows. If you had the right classroom you could
stare out the window, watching ships entering and leaving
the most magnificent harbor in North America. In the distance were the hills of Staten Island. If you peered up the
bay you could see the Statute of Liberty and lower Manhattan. I can even remember watching the Twin Towers taking
shape, and then how empty the vista looked after they came
crashing down in 2001. The Narrows always played on my
imagination. Even as a youth, I could not look at this body of
water without thinking about Giovanni da Verrazzano and
Henry Hudson heading their ships into a passageway from
the sea that surely would bring them to the Pacific. Many
times have I looked out at the ocean lapping onto the shore
and imagined the harbor in 1776 when the British sailed
a hundred ships into the Narrows with the largest expedi-
tionary force they would ever launch on the continent. I was
like the water gazers Herman Melville wrote about at the
beginning of *Moby Dick* – right after the "call me Ishmael"
bit – where he describes the landsmen "of the insular city

of the Manhattoes," who "must get just as nigh the water as they possibly can without falling in." There, then, was the real reason I headed to the shore in 1968. It wasn't just to get ready for my ride to Montreal; it was to let the sea and salt play on my imagination.

I took other rides as well in 1968. On weekends, Denis, Roger, and I might pedal past Coney Island and further along the bike path that parallels the Belt Parkway. We never had to push or try too hard. After all we were young. Later in the spring I began to ride with my friend Nina on a tandem bike she had bought with Denis. She and Denis had been dating for almost a year when they decided to go halvsies on the tandem. Inevitably they broke up with no court document to share custody of their joint purchase. Nina, who I had known since the seventh grade, turned to me for a riding partner. Being an independent and assertive young woman, she also insisted on riding in the front – no back seat for her. Once we even had a flat tire and Nina demanded that she should fix it.

Although I had my share of teenage angst, life in high school in 1968 was relatively benign. If anything, Fort Hamilton High School resembled Riverdale High in the Archie comic book series. Most of the people I knew didn't even drink alcohol. The only time I ever saw Denis imbibing liquor, for example, was that trip to the World's Fair when we were in junior high school. The "drug culture" had begun to creep into the school, but few of our immediate friends participated in it. The world of smoking dope and popping pills would become more prominent in the coming decades. There was, however, a larger cultural normalization of drug use in the sixties, especially as a part of the youth rebellion. Young people watched how their rock heroes sang paeans to drug use. Songs like "White Rabbit" (1967) by Jefferson Airplane became unofficial anthems to the drug culture. Among my crowd, Peter, Paul, and Mary's "Puff the Magic Dragon"

(1963) was a favorite. This normalization would have dramatic consequences which lingered for decades and remains in the opioid crisis of today.

By 1968 the great "sexual revolution" was in full swing. Every generation believes that it has discovered something new – sex. Of course, the joke has always been on young people since their parents obviously had discovered sex before them. Otherwise there would not be young people to make the discovery again. Heck, even premarital and extra-marital sex are not new. The rising divorce rate in the 1950s and 1960s attested to the extramarital sex. Premarital sex takes a little more work to prove. In lectures I would tell students that there were some New England towns on the eve of the American Revolution where one third of the brides were pregnant when they got married. Then I would challenge students to do a little genealogical digging, urging them to count the number of months between the marriage of their parents, uncles and aunts, grandparents, and even great grandparents and the birth of a first child to see if there was at least one example of verifiable premarital sex in their families. I'm not sure how many good Oklahoma college kids did the research, but those who did often reported to me that I was right. What was new in the 1960s was the emergence of the birth control pill. Approved by the FDA in 1960, by 1968 millions of women were using the pill and other contraceptive methods to avoid pregnancies, regardless of what the Pope or other religious authorities believed. With increased knowledge and usage of contraception, there emerged a cultural movement that encouraged sexual relations. One branch of this movement appeared in the objectification of the female body, best exemplified by the photographs in *Playboy Magazine*. Although Hugh Hefner proclaimed he supported complete personal freedom for both men and women, his main focus was on how women could please men. Another branch of this movement was embraced by young people on a more equal footing. Like generations before them, teenagers began to explore sexual relations sometime after puberty, but now they could do so in a culturally sanctioned way. They could also do so with less concern about the life changing implications of pregnancy, although, kids being kids, first timers often had coitus without effective contraception and premarital pregnancies continued to occur. Indeed, one of the long term implications of the sexual revolution was an increase in women having children outside of wedlock – a practice which today is common, but which in 1968 was rare. Having outlined the nature of the sexual revolution sweeping America in the 1960s, I must now confess a gap between the larger trends in history and my personal experience – my own participation in this cultural movement before the bike ride to Montreal was limited.

There was also a disjunction between my personal experience in high school and the problems confronting the wider world. I was aware of the global troubles, yet all too often I remained focused on my own little universe of friends and activities. Almost every night I sat in the living room with my parents and viewed the horrors of the Vietnam War unfold. Like everyone else, the Tet Offensive surprised me. Similarly, I watched with anticipation the siege of Khe Sahn, where 7,000 American marines held off tens of thousands of Viet Cong in a protracted battle that lasted 77 days. I had some friends and acquaintances who had older siblings fighting the war, but no one in my immediate family was involved. Both my brother and I were planning on attending college and would have 2S deferments. Surely, by the end of our college years, the war would be over. It was only after the Montreal ride, and as I faced graduation, that the war became real for me. Some of my classmates were more tuned into the problems of the globe. One young woman who was in several of my classes became obsessed with the starvation

and death in southeast Nigeria. She led the school's effort
to collect money to help feed the "starving children" there.
At the time I scoffed at her efforts, believing that the only
children who would be fed were the ones drafted into the Biafran Army. Looking back, I admire her, wishing I had taken
her charity more seriously. Given the genocide occurring in
half a dozen different countries today, we could use more
young "do-gooders" now.

I should also have been more interested in the student
and civil rights movements. By 1968, the call for civil rights
had been in the news for over a decade and student protest had been broiling on college campuses ever since the
free speech movement in Berkeley, California in 1964. Mid-
dle-class white students built upon the example of the civil
rights movement and the non-violent tactics of the Rever-
end Martin Luther King, Junior. Together these two forces
gathered momentum in the 1960s, especially with the civil
rights march on Washington for Jobs and Freedom in 1963
and the first major anti-war march on Washington in 1967.
In both instances, hundreds of thousands of Americans protested to demand change. My high school was integrated,
but remained about eighty percent white. For the most part
white and black students got along and as far as I knew there
was no overt racial tension. But there were also few minority
students in the more advanced classes, an issue that should
have been addressed. There were high school students in
1968 that joined in the civil rights and student protests. Fort
Hamilton remained peaceful, and that was fine with me at
the time. Again, looking back at my teenage self, I wish I had
been more active protesting something – almost anything.
There was an obvious social injustice in class assignments
and we had an autocratic principal who allowed us very little
freedom to express ourselves. I just was not ready to be an
agent of revolution.

I missed out on a movement that had an international

dimension. Young people in a wide array of countries were demanding change. Demonstrations broke out in Paris in May 1968 decrying capitalism, consumerism, the De Gaulle government and American imperialism. Strikes and disturbances, led by students and workers, then erupted across France, bringing the country almost to a stop. Similar, if less spectacular, protests erupted in Germany, Italy, Spain, Brazil, Mexico, and elsewhere. There was a brief effort of protest in Poland, and the short-lived democratization movement in Czechoslovakia was in part triggered by student action. In almost all of these countries the protestors were confronted by heavy-handed suppression and a ponderous mainstream society which did not understand why young people were taking to the streets, occupying buildings, and expressing themselves so vociferously. Each of these groups was independent of one another, but were aware that they were a part of a larger left-leaning international movement. There is no comparable left wing youth movement today. Instead, the right wing seems to be more transnationally active in the so-called populists movements that contributed to Donald Trump's electoral victory in the United States, the Brexit vote in the United Kingdom, and the anti-immigrant sentiment in France, Germany, Italy, Poland, Hungary, and elsewhere.

In the spring of 1968, Americans turned their attention to Morningside Heights where a protest over the building of a gymnasium by Columbia University led to the occupation of several college buildings and the suspension of classes. Black and white students opposed the university's use of public land that should have been reserved for poor African Americans in Harlem. Questions of free speech, as well as the war in Vietnam, also came into play. This conflict reflected what the president of Columbia, Grayson Kirk, called the generation gap. The attitude of many students was best summarized in, of all places, the movie *Planet of the Apes* (1968), when Charlton Heston (aged fifty-five and then a

liberal in politics) advised some young rebellious chimpan-
zees "don't trust anyone over thirty." Long hair and unshaven
faces became symbols of the youth rebellion, as epitomized
in the successful musical *Hair* (1968). My father watched
the Columbia demonstrations on television in disbelief. He
could not understand how anyone privileged enough to get
a higher education could behave like that. As far as he was
concerned, young people in college – he had only finished
the eighth grade in Norway – should happily focus on their
studies. His attitude reflected the approach of many working-class whites of his generation, as became all too apparent in confrontations between hardhats and long hairs and
when New York's police, batons swinging, forcibly removed
the Columbia protestors.

Although college campuses are relatively peaceful in
2018, the legacies of both the Civil Rights movement and
student protests from the sixties remain with us today. The
idea of popular demonstrations and mass marches has become embedded in the American political process. On January 20, 2018, well over a million and half people participated in cities across the nation in the second annual Women's
March to clamor against the policies of the Trump administration. Teenagers gathered hundreds of thousands for the
"March for Our Lives" on March 24, 2018, to oppose gun
violence after yet another mass shooting in a high school.
Nearly every incident where the police kill an unarmed black
person brings shouting protesters into the street as a part of
the Black Lives Matter movement.

* * *

If there was much history being made in 1968 – history
that remains with us today – my own life was focused on
more personal goals. As a part of our effort to get ready for
our summer adventure, Denis, Roger, and I took a practice
ride to Bear Mountain for an overnight in April. Well, not
really to Bear Mountain. Rather we stayed at a state park

near Lake Welch, just a few miles south and west of Bear Mountain. The idea was to see how we liked being on the road and how the camping would work out. I took my own bike, and Denis and Roger rode on the tandem. Since I had no fenders and no place to put much of anything, we loaded the tandem with our joint gear. We over packed. Denis decided that he would carry a cast-iron frying pan to cook our dinner and we lugged along several cans of Dinty Moore beef stew. We heated the stew in the cans, and ate our meal half warm. No matter. Our gourmand preparation meant that we did not have to clean the frying pan. That was just as well since the campground was officially closed and there was no running water. We jerry-rigged the pup tent on a wood framed camp site intended for a much larger canvas covering. The size of the tent was a great idea – small, light weight and easy to carry. Three teens in a tent was perfectly fine with us. Denis got the middle, while Roger and I were on either side. It was Denis's tent. The sleeping bags were a no-go. We would just take a blanket on the big trip, which, after all, would be in the summer.

Using the old methods of calculation – looking at a map, adding up the segments listed along the lines of the route – in 1968 we thought that the distance to Lake Welch was 63 miles. MapQuest today says it is just under 50 miles, while Google Maps has the distance as 53 miles. Google Maps also informs me, as I remembered anyway, the route was hilly. On the way to our destination, we climbed 2077 feet and coasted 1188 feet downhill (all of this precision is thanks to current technology). Starting near sea level, we ended at an altitude of 968 feet. Back then, and ever since, I came to understand what I call Gilje's First Gravitational Law of Bicycling: what goes down, must go up. Or, if you were enjoying your coast downhill, inevitably you would be soon struggling uphill. From my parents' house we followed Fourth Avenue, to Flatbush Avenue and crossed over the Brooklyn Bridge. Turning north on Sixth Avenue, we caught Broadway at Columbus Circle, and followed the Great White Way until we could connect with the George Washington Bridge (another hill). Google Maps wants any would-be biker today to cross the Hudson on a ferry. That would be fine with me since there is no pedaling on a ferry, especially one that angles up the river (Ah, there is more of the difference in mileage). In 1968 there were no ferries on the Hudson, so we had no choice: the only way to cross the river was the George Washington Bridge. You cannot ride a bike in the Lincoln or Holland Tunnels. We then headed north along the Palisades, connecting to Route 9W. Along the way we were treated to fantastic views of the Hudson. We stopped at one roadside restaurant in Grand View-on-Hudson (that is the accurate name of the town) and we each bought two pieces of pie (as teenage boys we never gave a thought to how many calories we ingested). This was the first time I tasted peach pie – the restaurant was out of apple and blueberry, my staples. Thereafter, peach became my pie of choice. Every time I have a slice of peach pie, I still think of that restaurant. We sat there and savored our two pieces of pie with the entire Hudson River Valley below.

Google Maps says the bike ride should take five hours and twenty seven minutes. We took all day. By the time we arrived, we were pretty tired. We were also surprised that the campground was closed. No one had thought to check before we left. However, we just picked up our bikes, despite the cast iron pan, cans of Dinty Moore, and cumbersome sleeping bags, and climbed over the chain blocking the road. We ate our partially heated canned dinner and felt a little miserable. Amazingly, miles from anywhere, there was a functioning phone booth. Using a dime, we called our parents collect. My dad offered to drive that evening to pick us up, throwing the bikes into the old station wagon. We declined. After all, it was going to be more downhill than uphill the next day. No need for Google Maps to tell us that.

On the return we took advantage of those downhills and, although our low tech bikes had no speedometer, we *know* that at one point we hit 45 miles per hour.

We learned a great deal on that trip. Cast-iron pan, no. Pup tent, yes. Sleeping bags, no. Blankets, yes. Dinty Moore Beef stew, no. Food as we needed (think peach pie), yes. And most important, we were ready for Montreal!

* * *

It was more work to get in shape in 2018. I had to make sure that my body would survive the training. First of all, I had to get my hands in shape. Hands? What do hands have to do with biking? Well, gripping the handle bars can make an old person's hands go numb. Twenty years ago my friend Rob, who was not then even that old, did the RAG-BRAI across Iowa and so injured his hands that he could not hold a tennis racquet for months – a serious tragedy for this ex-college player who shapes his daily schedule around his tennis games. My own hands were a big question mark. I was especially worried about my left hand. When I was fourteen my family's dog, a huge German Shepard named

Wolf – we affectionately called him Wolfie – had been so excited to see me standing by our front door as he returned from a walk that he charged, really galumphed, toward me and jumped on my back with love and affection. He sent me flying straight into a storm door which shattered and cut my left hand in several places. I ended up with six stitches. The biggest cut was on the palm of my hand under the thumb. I still have the scar. The most destructive cut was smaller in the middle of my palm. The nerves in that hand never fully recovered and the hand gets numb or "falls asleep" with all too much ease. If I slam the hand on the table, or just hold it in the wrong position, all these many years later I can feel it tingle. When I ride, every twenty minutes or so I need to take my hand off the handle bar and open and close the hand, just to be on the safe side.

I had to watch my back, since I struggled with back troubles on and off for forty years. My first back spasm occurred in my twenties when I was in graduate school. Since I was only a graduate student with minimal daily obligations, I simply rested for a few days and I was as good as new. But in my thirties, as my life became crammed with employment and family, and the tensions and worry of getting tenure, I experienced more spasms. I had to give up basketball because every time I played my lower back hurt and I listed to one side for a few days. Then there were the spasms. One occurred the day before a semester started when I was doing a jigsaw puzzle to relax. I reached awkwardly to place a piece into the puzzle and pain shot through the lower back. I shouted and collapsed to the floor unable to move. The kids were frightened and Ann thought I had a heart attack. We went to the emergency room as soon as I could move. Ever since, I do a hundred stomach crunches in the morning as well as other contortions as my inflexible body allows.

A bad back is not all bad. Over the years it became a great excuse to limit my activity around the house. I established my four hour rule: never work on any household project for more than four hours at a time. It also was a great way to create a little personal space. Not even the kids could argue when I said "Daddy needs to rest his back and lay down for a little bit – we can play later." Having believed for a minute that she was going to be a widow in her mid thirties, and having witnessed me incapacitated, even Ann bought the excuse. Fortunately, and perhaps because of the daily stretching, as I aged my back seemed to get better. The devastating spasms disappeared. In their place came soreness and some stinging pain. I therefore kept to the four hour rule and made sure that I rested whenever I felt a bit of a twinge. The four hour limit, the back stretches, the laying down, and the improvement with age were not enough. Two and a half weeks into my regimen of exercise to prepare for the ride, and in the midst of getting settled after our move to Philadelphia, I bent down to help lift a file cabinet into my car and felt a sharp dagger thrust into my lower left side. There was my back. I did not do any riding for several days and spent even more time than normal laying on my back waiting for my body to heal. I even despaired and began to wonder if I could do the ride. To make matters worse, it rained for over a week. After three days of not running or riding, I went to the stationary bike in the gym. No one was using it, no one had just used it, and no one was about to use it. I pedaled for forty-five minutes. I was going to get back in shape after all. Or was I?

I was also concerned with my heart. Heart problems run in my family. When I turned sixty, I had a heart scare. I jogged in part to fight genetics and, despite, or rather maybe because of, the eleven minute miles, I was in fairly good shape for an old guy. I only weighed twenty pounds more than when I started my senior year in high school, and I ran hundreds of miles a year. At my annual physical, when my regular doctor suggested a treadmill test to set a benchmark

for the future, I said, "bring it on." At that test the tech-
nicians were amazed, or at least that is what my ego told
me. I ran uphill for fourteen minutes before my heart rate
broke 140 beats per minute. Two weeks later I went to the
cardiologist to get the final result a day after my big six-o
bash. I was ready to hear the good doctor proclaim me a
regular superman, capable of running forever, if not able to
leap tall buildings. Instead, he asked in his Pakistani accent,
"how does your heart feel?" My hearing was not as strong as
it used to be and I was unsure what he was saying. I asked
him to repeat his question. "Oh, how does my heart feel? Just
fine! Why?" He replied, "There was an abnormality in the
test and I suspect you might have a blockage." "A blockage?
Certainly not." I thought for a minute. Real athletes had had
blockages. The great running guru Jim Fixx had died at age
51 of a heart blockage and he ran ten miles a day at a pace
faster than eleven minute miles. The doctor wanted to do an
angiogram. That is, he wanted to shove a tube up my artery
in my leg and peer into my heart searching for blockages. I
was thunderstruck. I was in shock. I had the test.

The good news was I had no blockage. The bad news
was that I had an enlarged heart. The doctor told me this in
recovery. Ann, who was with me, asked for details. Unper-
turbed by my condition, and unaware of our panic, the good
doctor informed us he would explain it all in my follow up
in two weeks. As soon as we got home, Ann did what you
should never do concerning a health issue. She looked it up
on the internet. Having an enlarged heart meant anything
from needing a heart transplant yesterday, to no big deal,
and everything in between. She did not know what to think,
and therefore imagined the worst. As I lay recuperating from
the procedure and anesthetic watching inane movies on the
television, Ann did not tell me of her findings. Instead, she
told me not to google "enlarged heart." She walked out of
the room and I immediately grabbed my laptop. What I

found was such a shock that it almost gave me a heart attack. Since I had scheduled the test for Friday, we did not call for further clarification until Monday. That weekend, I became convinced I was about to kick the bucket any minute. I did not. As it turns out, I have a *slightly* enlarged heart and merely had to make sure I did not overstress it.

I asked the doctor what caused my heart to enlarge slightly. He, being a devout Muslim, said it was probably from drinking alcohol. This was a low blow. I had admitted on my medical questionnaire to having a beer a few nights a week, and said I even had two some nights. Which is the truth. I suspect that doctors typically multiply by a factor of four whatever a patient admits to drinking. He advised me to stop drinking. This news was devastating. For my sixtieth, Ann had asked the seventy or so guests to bring a bottle of their favorite craft beer as a present. Several of my friends brought me six packs, a few even handed me two six packs – those are real friends. I had 248 bottles of beer in the fridge, representing 47 varieties of craft beer ranging from Belgian imports to the produce of the best West Coast breweries. There were beers that cost twenty dollars a bottle! Now, ironically I was supposed to give up my drinking so my heart did not become too enlarged. I could not follow that advice. Fortunately, my regular doctor was fine with me having a beer and even sometimes two. She said that my heart probably became enlarged from a lifetime of exercise and that athletes like Lance Armstrong (sans the drugs) had enlarged hearts. I did follow the cardiologist's advice on another matter. After turning sixty, I began to think about doing a marathon since I had skipped this long distance race in my younger and stronger days of running. When I asked the cardiologist for his opinion on the matter, he said that I should not put my body under that stress, although I could continue to run three or four miles at a time (just like I could have a beer or two a night, I thought). In other words, I had a doctor's note:

no marathon for me. What a relief. I did not ask him about a six-day bike ride. I did not want a doctor's note for that one.

Besides worrying about my hands, back, and heart – things I did not even think about in 1968 – there were the medical unknowns. I knew all about them. The heart scare had been an unknown. And there might always be some cancer or disease lurking deep inside me. The older you get, the more you see one friend after another plagued with health problems or stricken by some fatal disease, the more convinced you become that your body is a ticking time bomb ready to explode. When you are seventeen you are immortal; when you are sixty-seven, not only are you a mere mortal, you are painfully (literally and figuratively) aware of that mortality. The time to get ready, the time to hop on that bike, was now! The end is coming, and it is coming all too soon. Beyond whatever organ was ready to fail, and whatever growth might be developing, there were the muscular problems. The shoulder injury and the butt injury reminded me of how vulnerable my endoskeleton had become. Pacing and building strength were my goals.

Chapter 4

Finding a Riding Partner

A ROADBLOCK TO my jubilee tour to Montreal was finding a riding partner. Ann was fine with me taking the trip as long as I was not riding by myself. And there was the rub. Ann loves to bicycle and together in recent years we have done several rides of up to 45 miles: two Five Borough rides in New York City, a Tour de Brooklyn, the Lehigh Valley Trail, and countless shorter cycling excursions in Oklahoma, Philadelphia, and New York City. But six days on a bike was more than she bargained for when she married me forty five years ago.

I asked Rob, who was my best friend at the university to join me. Rob and I had both arrived in Oklahoma in 1980. We immediately hit it off. He studied the history of the United States in the twentieth century and I studied the American Revolution. Over the years, Rob and his wife, Ellie, became almost like family. We relied upon each other whenever there was something that needed to be done. When my daughter was born, Rob and Ellie took care of our four-year-old son. Fourteen years later, I took their teenage son to a specialist for his broken hand when Rob and Ellie were out of town. At the same time we built our careers together. Rob and I earned tenure and were promoted in the same years. In the late 1990s Rob became department chair and concentrated on administration. I headed the graduate committee, but focused more on research. Together we molded the department into the 2010s. Most importantly, we liked to pal around together. On our last day in Norman, Rob was there with his pick up – I had sold mine at a discount to Rob's son – for runs to the dump and Habitat for Humanity as we emptied our house before closing.

If I had to choose anyone to do the ride, it would have to be Rob. Like me, Rob commuted daily to campus on his bike. He had also gone on the Iowa RAGBRAI twice some twenty years ago. So he had some experience on long distance bike riding. He had been a college athlete who continued to work constantly on keeping in shape. Two inches taller, he weighed ten pounds less than me. We used to run together daily, but bad knees had forced him to give up the pounding of jogging. He played tennis several times a week and loved to ski in the winter. In short, he is in great physical shape. One evening, after several glasses of wine, Rob was all gung ho about the ride and agreed to join me. Even more important, Ellie was also all for the trip, planning on exploring the Hudson River Valley with Ann, while Rob and I rode our bikes up the river and into the Lake Champlain Valley. If Rob might waiver in a more sober moment, Ellie would push him to fulfill the commitment. Then Rob's knees hobbled him. With a possible knee replacement on the horizon, he was out of the picture for the summer of 2018.

* * *

So I turned to my backup. I had already discussed the trip with another Oklahoma running buddy, David, who was also an avid bike rider. In fact, I had already asked him to be backup if Rob fell through. David is perhaps the nicest person I know. An engineer, he is a top researcher in waste water and thus the *butt* of my best scatological humor. David also dedicated much of his life to doing good. He established a water center at the university, created an international prize for the best water research in engineering, and traveled the world in his effort to spread knowledge about how to obtain clean water. The guy has visited rural villages in Ethiopia, Cambodia, Bolivia, and a host of other countries I would not dream of traveling to. In short, he is a candidate for saint-hood. Although he is altruistic to the core, he also gained plenty of accolades along the way, including an endowed chair and multiple awards from the university, the state, and national organizations.

David is an odd mixture of humility and fierce com-petitiveness. Over the nearly thirty years we ran together, I watched David as he struggled to keep his competitive genie in the bottle. His humility compelled him to defer gracious-ly to Rob when we discussed the ride. His competitiveness reared its head anyway. He may have accepted being the sec-ond fiddle for the ride, but all through the fall and the spring, he reminded me each week of how many miles he *rode* on his *bike* on Saturday and Sunday. That's okay, I am from Brook-lyn and I could handle innuendo and a few slams now and then.

Besides, for decades *I* had been on the offensive. I was forever comparing our research records and noting that I had obtained a research professorship David once coveted. David of course, had earned a whole string of titles, includ-ing a professorship that reflected achievement in teaching, research, and service to the university. He also was granted an endowed chair. None of this stopped me. I was never one for not touting my own achievements. I would tell him of my latest book. David would then let slip how many publi-cations he had in a year, the record was 21, and that he had co-authored books as well. I, in turn, would needle him that as an engineering professor, his graduate students did all the research and writing and he just plunked his name on the publication at the end. At first, David would wince, and as a small town Illinois boy he tried to explain to me that the research projects had been his idea, that they were funded with his grants, and that he had to rework the prose since so many of his graduate students were non-native English speakers whose language skills needed his editorial hand. In short, he protested too much. After a decade or so, David got into the spirit and learned that every time I threw some "chum" at him that he could snap at, he would either retort in kind, or just ignore me and keep on telling his story.

Since I was older and clearly wiser, I never hesitated to give David advice on our runs. As David liked to say, he always listened to my advice, and even occasionally followed it. One day twenty years ago, David told me that he and his wife, Frances, had been discussing buying a camper. Without giving him a chance to say another word, I launched into a long diatribe on all the reasons buying a camper was a bad idea – waste of money, maintenance and storage issues, better to rent for the time you actually needed it, his wife would hate camping, etc. etc.. Every half mile or so David attempted to get a word in edge wise, with a "But Paul . . .". I would cut him off and continue with my rant. Nothing stops me once I get into a good rant. After five miles of running, I had exhausted my arguments. David then finally finished the sentence he had tried to get out for the entire run. "But Paul, Frances and I already bought the camper."

David was religious. Whenever I faced some problem – when you run with someone decade after decade, you share almost everything – he promised he would pray for me. He had been born Lutheran like me, but had abandoned the high-church world in college and attended a mega church in town. A conservative with a strong social conscience, David was pro-life and often quoted the Bible. In a good Christian spirit, I forgave David these faults.

His biggest fan is his wife Frances. She is Southern through and through. Born in Tennessee, Frances is a genuinely good person. She loves her house and Norman, and does not join David on his more exotic trips. She did spend a year in Germany with him on a sabbatical when their kids were young and recently joined him for a month of teaching in Arezzo, Italy. She prefers to vacation closer to home and every summer David and Frances drove to Colorado for a week in the mountains. She accepts, understands, and supports David's travels to distant parts to save humanity. She also has a nice sense of humor. As a son of the land of Lincoln, David has a passion for all things belonging to and about "Honest Abe." He has read every biography on Lincoln and collects Lincoln memorabilia. One day about fifteen years ago, David turned to me on a run and proudly, as proud as his own humility would let him go, proclaimed that he had just bought a lock of Lincoln's hair and, anticipating my response, said he had documentation to prove it was real. Personally, I view the possibility that this lock of hair was authentic, as likely as the millions of holy splinters circulating the globe were actually pieces of the true cross. So the devil rose up in me. I asked him if the lock was curly, and if so, might it not be strains of Lincoln's pubic hair. When David repeated my comment to Frances, she laughed and later told me that every time she walks past the framed strands of hair, she thinks of me and has to smile.

Frances may have considered my jibe clever, and possibly true, but ultimately she thinks the world of her husband. In this she differed from my wife. Ann loves me dearly, but knows all too well my shortcomings and is not averse to pointing them out. Shortly before Ann and I left Norman for good, David and Frances invited us over for dinner. The food was great and the company even better. Somehow the conversation had turned to our dead parents. Frances, in her sugary Southern drawl, said that her father had died six months before her mother and that it was almost as if when her "Daddy" got to heaven, he lobbied the powers that be for "Mama" to join him. It was an endearing thought and a bit too saccharine for my tastes. I had to make a quick riposte and turned to Ann and told her, "if you go first, whatever you do, don't lobby for me to join you. Because as soon as you kick the bucket, all of these younger women – and by younger I mean women in their fifties – will be all over me." Without missing a beat, Ann responded, "You're delusional!" We all laughed. Frances then told David, in all sincerity, that when (not if) she dies before him, he would make a wonderful husband for another woman. David gasped, and said, "Dear, I already thought I was a wonderful husband." "Of course you are, David."

Despite his slightly rotund belly and bald pate, David is a real athlete. As a teenager he was a high school runner who clocked a four and a half minute mile. Now, of course, he is an eleven minute miler (on a good day) with me. Whatever his current running condition, he is a serious biker, putting in, as he reported on every Monday morning, scads of miles on the weekend. He also does several group rides each year, including the Hotter'N Hell 100 in Texas – a late August ride that is 100 miles long and in temperatures that usually hit over 100 degrees. Anyone willing to ride that distance in those conditions, surely would be willing to ride with me on the trek to Montreal. The majestic Hudson, the deep blue of Lake Champlain, the Adirondacks in the distance, would be far more interesting and picturesque than the hot, dusty, and windy plains of Wichita Falls. Sure, he would have to take off a week from teaching (he is six years younger than me and not retired), but that would not be a problem. He is, after all, a tenured and endowed college professor. To be on the safe side, I asked Randy, his department chair and another running buddy, to let David go. Manipulator that I am, I also asked Randy to join us. He gave his official assent to David's missing a week of work, and was willing to go along with us until his own wife told him that there was no way with five kids (he is Catholic) that he could miss a week of after school activities. As far as Randy was concerned, though, David could still go. Unfortunately, David began to waver. He led me to believe that he was too conscientious of his academic responsibilities and that he did not relish the idea of losing a week in the classroom. He also had another scenic Hotter'N Hell to do.

* * *

Ever since I first thought about redoing the trip, in the back of my mind was the possibility of contacting my old high school companions. I had not been in touch with either of them for twenty-five years. I last saw Denis sometime in the 1980s when he had visited me in Oklahoma as he traveled cross country. When you live in a flyover state, few people ever visit you. The fact that Denis did, meant that either he had no place better to go, or that he was willing to go out of his way to see me. Roger was a somewhat different story. I had kept in more regular contact with him through the 80s, and would see him whenever I went to Brooklyn. After my mother died in June 1992, my connection to Brooklyn weakened and it was several years before I made it back to my home turf. By then I had lost track of Roger and our lives went their separate ways. A few years ago, I learned that he had settled in Silver Springs, Maryland. After college he earned real money as a carpenter remodeling houses in New York. However, sometime in the 1990s he went to law school at the University of Arizona. If he drove there, which he probably did, he did not stop in Oklahoma to see us. From 1992 to 2017, Roger did not contact me. I did not contact him. With my riding partner options beginning to narrow, I called Roger. When we finally connected, we chatted for

over an hour as if nary a day had expired since last we talked. Roger did not turn me down outright. He was intrigued
with the idea of redoing the bike ride, although he confessed
that he had not ridden longer than five miles at a time in
ten years. He left the door open though, and encouraged me
to contact Denis. I tried calling Denis multiple times. There
was never any answer at the phone number Roger gave me
and the message box was full. My efforts fell short. Roger
remained my best hope.

Before the end of May, Roger sent me the bad news.
Although he did not say it, I think he had been almost ready
to join me on the bike tour. When I had not heard from him
for a couple of weeks, I began to get antsy so I sent him a
follow up email. He responded a week later. His heart apparently was all a flutter with the idea of the ride. As he put it:
"Guess where I was when I read your email. Right, in an ER
waiting to find why my heart was beating like a busted toy."
He had experienced his first "afib event." This condition is
marked by an irregular heartbeat that results from the upper
two chambers of the heart not contracting in conjunction
with the lower two chambers, often setting the pulse racing
way too fast. Fortunately for Roger, just as he lay on the gur-
ney to be sent in for an electric shock to re-coordinate the
chambers of his heart, the heartbeat came into sync on its
own. They sent him home, but he experienced several lesser
"events" thereafter. He did not shut the door completely on
the bike ride, but he did not think it likely. Nor did I. I began
to wonder if I would find a riding partner, and as I struggled
with my own physical ailments, I concluded that this getting
old business was no fun.

* * *

After Roger's email, I was desperate and tried David
again. I gave him the hard sell, although I was convinced it
would be a fruitless effort. To my surprise, David suddenly
was not only willing, but eager to go. In his own humble way,

he credited me with my sales pitch. He said that when he shared my latest email with Frances, she had told him I was "quite the salesman." He also admitted that there would be another Hotter'N Hell next year as well. In reality, he had been chomping at the bit all along, and had only held back to make sure that my high school buddies could not make it before throwing his biking helmet into the ring. Using airline miles, David quickly obtained plane tickets and he and I began to exchange daily emails about the plans. Frances would join Ann in the sag wagon and the two of them would

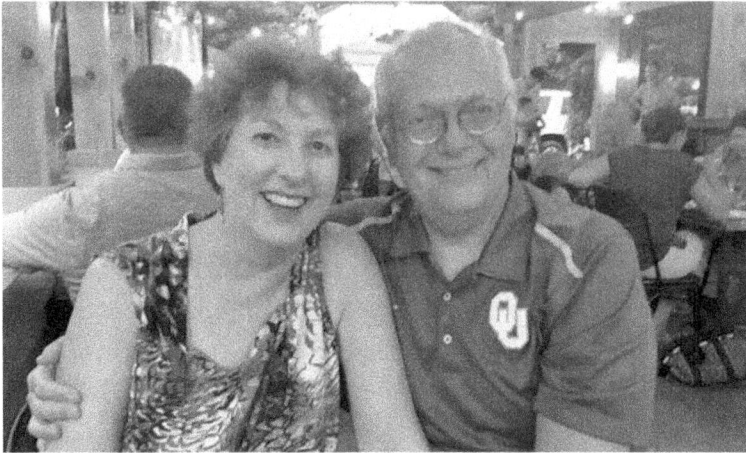

tour the Hudson River Valley. We might have to pray at every meal with David and Frances, but given the larger endeavor, a little prayer might not be a bad thing. David in the meantime had used Google Maps to measure how much uphill and downhill we would travel. He ordered New York and Canadian biking jerseys for the first and last day, apologizing for not finding a jersey with Montreal on it. Of course I had to order the same jerseys so we could look like a team. David was thinking of the photo opportunities. Suddenly the trip was really on, and just as suddenly I knew I had to train in earnest.

Chapter 5

Equipment

THE PARTNER THING settled, I turned my thoughts to getting the right equipment. On this trip there would be no pup tent and certainly no frying pan – hotels and comfort were the watchword. As I had explained to Roger, "The way I see it, if it is 400 miles to Montreal from Brooklyn, then all we have to do is 67 miles a day for six days. At 10 miles an hour (an easy pace for sure), that is less than seven hours a day. There would be no biking into the middle of the night. We would put in our 67 miles, call the sag wagon driven by our wives and go to a hotel. We wouldn't need a map, nor look for a phone booth. We would have our cell phones for instant communication and a constant GPS reading. We could even take showers every day and eat in a restaurant. Piece of cake [or maybe pie] right?" All we had to carry was some emergency food, drinks for the day and the standard bike accouterments.

* * *

Back in 1968, as Roger correctly remembered, our outfits were "pretty rudimentary." But he also misremembered what we wore. He described our clothing as "Cutoff shorts, jeans, t-shirts, and tighty whities." He only had the tighty-whites correct. As a group picture at the beginning of the ride reveals, we had on neither cutoffs nor tee shirts. Denis and I have on ordinary shorts (Roger might have had cutoffs, but I doubt it). Denis wore a collared pull over shirt. Roger actually sported a plaid long sleeve button down shirt with collar, and a bandana tied around his neck. I wore a top similar to a tee shirt that was called a polo shirt in those days. It was made out of terry cloth and had stripes. Roger's comments highlight a dramatic sartorial shift that began in the 1960s and might be called the "casual revolution" – a part of the youth rebellion that brought us the more recognized "sexual revolution" and "drug culture."

Take tee shirts for example. In 1968, few people wore this now familiar unisex top with emblems and wording. White tee shirts had long been used as underwear and might be seen when men removed their shirts to labor at hard tasks. In the 1950s, after Marlon Brando and James Dean appeared in movies in white tee shirts, wearing an undershirt in public became more popular. But what we would recognize as the modern tee shirt was rare. In the early 1960s there was some effort to sell tee shirts with images on them. The Rock and Roll Hall of Fame displays an Elvis Presley tee shirt from the early sixties, but the museum label notes that it was not very popular since it was considered a "cheap" souvenir of the period's greatest teen idol. There were also a few vacation destinations in Florida and elsewhere that sold tee shirts advertising their facilities. Their use, however, was not widespread. Only as the late 1960s gave way to the early 1970s did the tee shirt become popular. This shift resulted from a combination of changes in technology in silk screening and in the desire of many young people to trumpet their favorite rock band on their clothing. Even by the time you get to Woodstock (1969), there were only a handful of tee shirts with logos and designs emblazoned on them. Images from this iconic rock festival reveal young men who are shirtless, wearing white undershirts, polo shirts (old style), or regular collared shirts. There are only a few tops we would recognize as the modern tee. In 2018, tee shirts are everywhere and are considered acceptable clothing for almost any occasion. Only the most exclusive restaurants will insist on a collared shirt, tie, and jacket. Cheap and comfortable, the average American owns at least ten tee shirts. When I checked my high school year book, the only tee shirts that appeared in any of the pictures were from gym class. You can also get a sense of the formality of clothing in the 1960s by looking at the teachers: the women all wore nice dresses and the men donned jackets and ties. The "casual revolution" loosened things up dramatically. Now, unless there is a dress code or uniform, over half the students in high school and college wear tee shirts. Many don baseball caps. In 1968, only people playing baseball, or a real rube like Gomer Pyle, wore a baseball cap. College professors also dress down. Some even wear tee shirts to class. Not me. I always put on a tie and often wore a sports jacket. In fact, I had a different tie for every day I taught, usually with pictures depicting some historical theme connected to the day's lecture.

There is an upside to the casual revolution that became apparent when I was a senior in high school. Although there were no overtly political protests at Fort Hamilton that year, there were individual actions of civil disobedience by several young women who objected to the dress code preventing them from wearing pants even in the cold of winter. By 1968 women wearing pants had become commonplace in casual situations, but in our high school the principal was dead set against the practice, deeming pants inappropriate attire for girls and too sexually suggestive. How completely covering ones legs was more suggestive than a skirt that rose several inches above the knee – this was the era of the mini-skirt – is beyond me. Asserting that pants could ward off the frigid blasts of winter wind better than panty hose and a skirt, several young women decided to ignore the dress code. At first, the administration simply sent the girls home to change. One of my classmates said that she was sent home nine separate times. Persistence began to pay off when the principal allowed the girls to wear pants under their skirts as long as they removed the pants once they arrived at school. Eventually the absurdity of this position became too obvious, and the principal allowed young women to don pants in cold and inclement weather. Later, after we graduated from high school, young women were allowed to wear pants at any time. This was just as well, since pants became increasingly accepted even in business fashion. In 1969 Charlotte Reid became the first congresswoman to wear pants in the House of Representatives. By the end of 1968, fashion designers began to feature women's pantsuits for professional occasions. Even when she was first lady, Hillary Clinton preferred pants and as a senator, secretary of state, and presidential candidate, she made the pantsuit her normal attire. On election day in 2016, convinced that Clinton would coast to victory, many American women joined the "Pantsuit Nation" and wore Hillary's signature style as a show of solidarity.

* * *

If everyday clothing has changed since 1968, so too have biking outfits. Today, there are special bike pants with padding to protect your rear. I resisted wearing such pants for the longest time. Bike pants are made of spandex. As much as I admire watching young women squeezed into such body-clinging attire, I am a bit too flabby to be comfortable with doing the same. Ann convinced me otherwise by having me try on a set of riding pants which came with the spandex and padding beneath the ocular protection of a pair of shorts. In my ignorance I initially wore the inner pants with the padding backwards since the spandex and shorts were two separate items of clothing. Somehow the inner riding pants were hung on the rack with the back toward the front. I simply put them on the way they were arranged when we bought them. This thoughtlessness meant the extra padding reached up the front of my crouch insuring special coverage for my more delicate parts. The arrangement felt a bit awk-ward. I did not know any better and assumed that the idea was to offer genital protection if I slipped forward and hit the bar that ran from the front to the back on the bike. I was also amused by the thought that if anyone cared to stare at that part of my anatomy, they might have wondered at the size of my personal equipment bulging under my zipper. No one seemed to notice. After a few rides I figured out the error of my ways and began to enjoy the cushioning in its appro-priate place – my butt.

I more readily adopted a helmet. When I was nineteen, I had a brief motorcycle career. Crashing headfirst into a brick wall showed me the utility of wearing a helmet – without head protection the one inch hole chipped out of the helmet would have been taken from my skull. Still, it was not until the 1980s that I wore my first helmet on a bicycle. Today, I would not think of riding anywhere without one, just as I could not imagine driving in a car without a seatbelt. A few years ago Ann and I visited Amsterdam, one of our favorite cities in the world. We admired the bike culture there and stood agog as a woman pedaled past with one child in a car-rier on her handle bars and two others sitting behind her, while transporting groceries in sacks attached to the side. But no helmets. I asked the Dutch proprietor of our bed and breakfast about why so few people in Amsterdam wore helmets. He looked down at me (the Dutch are the tallest people in the world), and condescendingly and inanely ex-plained to me in his perfect English, that the Dutch grew up on bicycles and did not need helmets. They knew how to ride safely. I wanted to declare that I had grown up on a bicycle, had ridden to Montreal on one, and regularly commuted on one, and I wore a helmet. But I didn't. I thanked him for his answer and left it at that.

In 1968 everything I did was bare bones. As far as I know, there was no such thing as bicycle gloves back then.

If I wore gloves, it was because my hands were cold. I never had a light on my bike. You really didn't need one to ride in the city at night since there were street lamps galore. As I got older I came to realize that a bike light is not so the rider can see the road; rather it is so people driving cars can see the rider. Hence, bike lights come in two modes. One with the light constantly on; the other with it blinking to gain people's attention. I had no idea about reflective gear in those days. Today I have bike shirts in bright yellow that make me stand out like a canary in a coal mine. Ann also bought me suspender-like reflectors for those evenings I came home from the university after dark. Although I would struggle with getting the straps right, I even used them a few times. Today most cities have ordinances that all bikes should have a bell. I am all for such regulations. However, a bell is almost useless these days. Along popular biking and jogging paths, like the Schuylkill River Trail, ninety percent of the runners have ear buds with music blasting. I can ding-a-ling to my heart's content and the jogger remains oblivious. At least runners move in a straight line. On campus, where I have done much of my biking for decades, students now remain glued to their devices. As they pluck out their latest text on a walkway shared by bikes, they wobble back and forth in unpredictable trajectories. They too plug up their ears with buds that limit the incoming sounds around them. Oh well. Regardless, I have a bell and a light.

I have other gear as well. In 1968 I carried an old camping canteen for water on long trips. Strapped around my neck, I was lucky I did not choke myself to death. Now there are water bottles and nifty little water bottle holders attached to the bike frame. I eventually bought special insulated water bottles that would match the colors on my new bike. Bike shirts have pouches in the back for water bottles and handy snacks. Anything in that pouch was not particularly handy to me. My inflexible body does not allow me to reach behind my back while riding and whip out an energy bar or a drink of Gatorade. If I needed to quench my thirst or sate my hunger, I was just fine with stopping to get what I needed from elsewhere. You can also place a rack attached to the rear of a bike and use a saddlebag that snaps in and out of the rack. I have an additional carrier to hold books and papers that I can attach to the rack (for when I was working). Before I retired, with the bike rack and bags, as well as a backpack strapped to my shoulders, I could take reams of papers, a laptop, books, my lunch, and my running outfit with me as I commuted to and from the university. In addition to this equipment, of course, I have a speedometer and an odometer so I can know exactly how fast and how far I am going. It is all so civilized.

* * *

I also wanted to obtain the right bicycle. In 1968 I had what I called an English racer, with ten gears and curved handle bars. Of course the bike was made in America, and was really not much of a racer. My dad had bought me the bike for $43. It was manufactured by AMF (American Machine and Foundry), the company my dad had worked for (notice the tense) as a machinist.

Here it is appropriate to note a striking connection between 1968 and 2018. By the late 1960s the rust had begun to show in the great manufacturing belt that ran from the Northeast through the Upper Midwest. In 2016, Making America Great Again was all about returning to the heyday of American industrialization in the 1950s and 1960s. The changes that were beginning then had a direct impact on my family. My dad was an immigrant from Norway who came to Brooklyn in 1936. Donald Trump would have embraced his arrival, even though my dad's family was so poor in what was then a "s—hole country" (admittedly a beautiful "s—hole country) that they left the place of their birth to seek opportunity in a depression ridden United States. My dad started working for AMF before World War II and returned to the same factory in Marine Terminal, Brooklyn, after serving in the army as a draftee. The shop was union, which brought tremendous benefits to my family. Thanks to the union my dad earned a living wage with health and dental coverage for his whole family. Thanks to the union I grew up middle class and unlike my parents I finished high school and went off to college. Ultimately, it was this upbringing which allowed me to continue my education, earn a PhD and become a history professor. Even though I myself only belonged to a union once when I had a summer job with Western Union in 1969, I know fully that unions allowed me to become the person I am. Making America great cannot be pronounced from the top down by some politician/salesman. Rather, the success for white Americans in the mid twentieth century, a time when incomes were more evenly distributed than today, came from the bottom up. Whatever the success of unions, they often drove employers nuts. In 1967, the year before my bicycle ride, the workers in my dad's factory went on one strike too many. Fed up with New York unions, AMF fled the city for greener non-union pastures. My dad lost his job at age 48. My father eventually found a new job with the New York City Transit Authority repairing subways, a job with better pay and constant work. Moreover, his new employer, unlike AMF, would never relocate out of the city. As a historian, I also should note that my father's experience reflected a larger historical trend for the nation's economy: the shift from manufacturing to the service sector. Fortunately for me, he had bought the bicycle before the strike. Although my father lost his job in manufacturing, that bike was my pride and joy even if it was a bit of a clunker and a bit too small of a frame for my six foot body. This was the bike I took to Montreal.

I replaced that bike with a real English racer, a Raleigh Grand Prix. Ann and I bought matching bicycles the first year we were married. Both were large framed men's bikes, which despite Ann's long legs and her five foot ten inches, was always a little bit of a stretch for her. I held unto my Raleigh Grand Prix until we moved from Oklahoma early in 2018 when I sold it as "vintage" for $40 (Ann had already gotten rid of hers). I had bought each bike for $165 in 1974. About fifteen years ago I purchased a used Raleigh C-40, a so-called hybrid bike, that had the gear shift in the handle grips, rather than on the bar of the frame as in my previous two bikes. It also had straight handle bars. Shortly after Ann and I purchased our condo in Philly, we bought matching Trek Verve bikes together for around $500 each. These are wonderful bikes for riding in flat areas. They have cushy seats, plenty of gears, and even a suspension system that provides a comfortable, if sometimes too squishy a ride. But they are heavy with thick hybrid tires. It was difficult for me to push the bike more than 12 miles per hour. On any incline I can gear down so far as to travel almost effortlessly uphill, but at an absolute crawl. Climbing the Hudson Highlands, I feared, would be excruciatingly slow. The foothills of the Adirondacks would be a killer. I decided to purchase a new bike with a price range of somewhere between $1000 and $1500. But like getting started in the first place, I procrastinated. I came up with all sorts of reasons for putting the purchase off. If I was going to make that sort of investment, I *needed* to know for sure that the bike would suit me. And I *needed* to settle the outstanding variables of the trek: first that my body would hold up and second, that I could find a riding partner or partners to share the experience. On May 2, since I never got around to purchasing a new bike in the fall of 2017, I procrastinated some more, resolving to start with my Trek comfort bike and see where I was by June 1.

David's commitment to join me accelerated my shopping. I had gone to a few local bike stores back in 1968 for parts to repair my bike. They always seemed to be run by some little Italian guy with a strong accent. Today, hipsters rule in most bike stores. Indeed, going to a bike store is a lot like walking into an urban barber shop, where both the male and female attendants have strange haircuts and tattoos splayed all over the exposed parts of their bodies. Who knows what lurks on the unexposed parts of their bodies? This was as true in Norman, Oklahoma, as it was in Philadelphia, Pennsylvania.

Having grown up in New York City, I have a healthy skepticism of all salespeople. I was hoping for a somewhat different experience when I started shopping for a bike, assuming that the tattooed hipsters who worked there did so because they were both knowledgeable about bikes and interested in biking. I had specific criteria that I was looking for in a bike. Ideally I wanted some of the comforts of my Trek Verve, with the climbing ability and speed of a road bike. This may have been asking for too much. Comfort and biking efficiency may not work in tandem. I was up front with the salespeople and told them about my budget and that I wanted a bike that would be good for a sixty-seven-year-old man who would be traveling 400 miles in six days. Unfortunately, most of the salespeople just offered me what they carried in their shop and did not think about my particular needs. They heard my budget and came up with a road bike that might be close to what I was hoping to pay. Most would have made the same recommendation to a twenty-seven-year-old. Whereas I thought that my budget was ample and generous, it quickly became apparent to me that $1,500 had merely brought me a notch above the bottom of the line in the new bicycle world. This was a long way from my $43 AMF "racer" and $165 Raleigh Grand Prix.

I began my shopping in the fall in Norman. I needed some spokes replaced on my used Raleigh hybrid and when I picked up the bike I talked to the thirty-something owner of the shop, her name was Olga, who had both body piercings and tattoos. She advised that I get a road bike, arguing that my body would adjust and that the curved handle bars would give me three different positions to hold my hands: on the far end of the curved bars, half way up the bars, and on the cross bar. Olga also said that I could get handle bar extensions that could provide a more upright grip. She was fairly convincing. Road bikes, however, can go for more than $10,000. The only thing she focused on was my price range, which could either buy me a top end Cannondale CAAD Optimo 105 or a low end CAAD12 165. The two other road bike categories carried by Cannondale were out of reach entirely: the Supersix Evo began at $2,100 and went to $11,000 and the System Six began at $4,000 and went to $11,000. I can't even begin to explain what you get for all that money. Although she did not have either of her recommendations in the shop, she showed me pictures on the internet. I guess this is the modern way of shopping. You either buy an item on the internet, or go to a store where they show you what they can order on the internet. I test rode a similar bike (the name eludes me now) and I found the ride so stiff and uncomfortable that when I came back, all I could say was that it was a young man's bike. I put off the decision and concentrated on finishing my last semester of teaching.

Once David had his airline tickets in hand, I had to get serious about purchasing a new bike. The training miles I had put on with the Trek Verve only convinced me further that a new bike would allow me to zip along on the flats, push up any hill, and fly down the other side. In my head this new bike would make the whole trip a breeze. I really was delusional.

I should have shopped earlier and looked at more options. Instead I visited the local bike shop in my Philadelphia neighborhood and the Trek store where Ann and I bought the Verves. I wanted to purchase a bike from the local store. It would be so easy to get tune-ups and information, since every time I stepped out of the apartment it would be a hop, skip, and a jump away. It was a great store with plenty of customers, both old and young. It was packed with tattooed male and female mechanics working on tons of bikes. It was clearly a successful business. But I lost confidence in the salespeople. I got two different sets of recommendations from the store from two different hipsters on two different days. Mike, the first salesperson I met was very helpful. He gave me all kinds of training advice and sounded intrigued when I told him about my projected journey – pardon me, "road tour," which is apparently what this generation calls my planned multi-day ride. He wondered if I had allowed enough time to get ready for the trip, a concern that had already lodged in the back of my mind. Mike said I needed to slowly build up my miles and that I should not ride every day. He claimed that it was on the days off that your muscles get strengthened for the next batch of training. I liked that advice. This store specialized in Specialized, the brand. Mike urged me to get a road bike since I was going on a road tour. Like Olga, he merely highlighted two road bikes Specialized carried that were in my price range. The Amira SL4 and the Tarmac; both for $1600. As the Specialized webpage explains: "The base Tarmac brings performance to the masses, with many of the same technologies that you'll find in our higher-end models, but with a price tag that's a bit more palatable." How $1600 was "more palatable" remained unclear to me. The description goes on to discuss the "performance geometry," which meant that the bike frame and handle bars wanted my aging body to bend way further forward than I was comfortable with. He had neither bike in the store, but showed me pictures on the internet. At least the bikes were close to my budget. Mike was a straightforward honest kid who really was trying to help me. As a twenty-something he just did not get what I was looking for.

A week later Ann and I popped into the bike store together. We were in the process of giving our son and his wife our used Raleigh hybrids that we had moved from Oklahoma and Ann wanted to buy our daughter-in-law a child seat so she could tool around with our two-year-old grandson in tow. Having looked up all the details on the internet, Ann knew exactly what bike seat she wanted. Rather than order it on line and install it herself – which she is very capable of doing – she decided to order it through the bike store and pay $15 to have the shop install it properly. After all, the safety of our grandson was at stake. She bought the child seat from a different salesman, Ryan. Ryan was smooth. Ryan was smart. Ryan was a great salesman. Ryan was slick and slippery and if he did not have an answer, he made it up. In the process of buying the child seat, I asked Ryan what bike he thought I should get for my ride. He also showed me a road bike. The Robaix Elite for $2800 which was over a thousand dollars above my budget and featured "the all-new Future Shock 'suspension' system" which "at the cockpit delivers a revolutionary degree of comfort and control." I liked seeing the word "comfort" in the description. It just so happened that they had one of these in the store, so I took it on a test ride in the streets and even climbed the South Street bridge hill. There were no miracles. I still struggled to get up the hill. Maybe I just did not know how to work the gears. But some young person (another twenty-something) in a not particularly fancy bike passed me as I pedaled up the hill. I also did not like the "geometry" of the handle bars and I am not sure that the "suspension" system really provided the kind of cushion I thought I wanted. To be honest, I felt awkward on the bike and I probably did not give it a fair trial. Like many riders who have bikes with the curved handle bars (and I had had two such bikes in the past) I prefer to ride with my hands gripping the cross bar, which left the brakes too distant since they sat forward ahead of the racing bar. The bike is beautiful, and Ryan, ever the salesman, said I would turn heads with it. "Wow", I thought, "I could have a bike that turns heads." I liked that idea. But it was not for me. No problem, Ryan had another suggestion the Men's Sirrus Pro Carbon for $2400. It, too, had the new "future shock" suspension system. It had straight handle bars and better "geometry" for those interested in fitness. It looked like a great bike and I might have bought it right then, had there been one in the store to test ride. My budget was somewhat artificial and I set the $1500 target really to insure that the salespeople would not try to oversell me too much. Besides, David had said that I should be able to get a good bike for that price. I left the store half convinced that my shopping was done. Yet I was uncomfortable ordering the bike sight unseen, although Ryan assured me that this particular model was selling like hot cakes. I said I would think about it.

In the meantime, Ryan had ordered the child seat for Ann's old bike and decided to install it himself since he wanted to impress us. He had suggested that it might be two or three days before one of their mechanics could work on it and he probably thought that if he could get it to us immediately, I would be so dazzled that I would buy the high dollar Men's Sirrus Pro Carbon. Unfortunately, Ryan mis-installed the seat. He placed the bars of the new rear rack too close to the cables and had not read the instructions. As a result the child seat did not snap into place and could tilt back at about a 60 degree angle. When Ann showed Ryan that the seat could swivel front to back, he looked her straight in the eye and said that that is the way it is supposed to be. As he explained, with all the confidence in the world, the movement of the seat served as a suspension for the seat so the bumps would not be too hard on the babies bottom! This made no sense to us, since we could envision our grandson rocking back and forth and throwing our daughter-in-law off balance and the two tumbling to the ground. Ann was fuming. We picked up the bike and seat. When we got back to our apartment, Ann read the instructions, re-installed the bike seat so that it snapped into place. There was no way I was spending $2400 and buying a bike from Ryan.

Although it was in the suburbs and a bit of a drive, we decided to try the store where we bought our Verve comfort bikes. There we met Ray. As far as I know, Ray has no tattoos. He is probably in his early thirties and was once a serious biker. He sports curly hair that is just a tad too long, and carries a little too much weight around the middle. He is not a hard body rider. But he knows bikes and is a good mechanic. He was also a good salesperson who actually listened to me. I told him what I wanted and he provided options. He, too, suggested a road bike, but when I told him I did not feel comfortable on a road bike, he said that I was the one who was doing the riding and therefore whatever I wanted is what I should get. Ray suggested a high-end hybrid with straight handlebars. He showed me a Trek FXS-5. It had a carbon frame. It was lightweight and had disc brakes. However, the bike only had 20 gears and no front suspension. Ray did not tell me that there was another model with additional gears for a few hundred dollars more. Maybe he did not do so because the FXS-5 was already a little over my budget at $1700. Or maybe he had the FXS-5 in the store and wanted to move the one on inventory. Regardless, he told me right off that he would discount it by $150 to get it close to my budget – a shrewd sales move. I also got to test ride it. Yes, it was a little stiff. Yes, even for a hybrid I was bent over further than I wanted to go. Yes, it did not have a suspension system. But the clock was ticking. I bought the bike. Ray added handle bar extenders and a rack for the back. He also suggested a change to puncture resistant tires. I ended up spending around $2000 anyway (including the tax). At last, I had a new bike.

I also had Ray in my corner. Ray seemed genuinely excited about my ride. He suggested training strategies. We exchanged stories about races (mine were the running kind). Ray admitted that he had physically collapsed in a Colorado mountain bike tour because he had not eaten enough protein. I told him how I passed out at the end of one 10K race because I had not hydrated enough. Ray told me to return for a tune up before my Montreal trip. He also suggested that I could bring him a six pack of beer for an afterhours lesson on bike repair. I thought this one of those generous offers that neither of us really wanted to pursue. As it turned out, I did not give Ray a six pack and I did not get the repair lesson. Regardless. I liked Ray. He might have given me a load of bulls–t as he sold me the bike. But as I used to tell my colleagues whenever we had to write a report for the university administration, the best bulls–t is true bulls–t.

Chapter 6

Getting Serious

WITH DAVID ON board, I not only had to buy my bike quickly, I also had to get serious about preparing for the 400 mile trek. I had spent some time on my comfort bike, but now I had to build up my stamina, and my butt, so that I could do 67 miles a day for six days. It had all sounded so easy when I was trying to persuade others to join me. Suddenly it became too real. Like many a great idea, this one did not look so great close up.

I quickly came to realize that the ride was going to take over my life that summer. I needed to ride at least five days a week regardless of the weather. When a miserable heat wave hit Philadelphia in July, I woke up at 4:30 AM, long before dawn, ate breakfast and got out on the road before the sun and humidity brought the heat index to over 100. Naps in the afternoon helped compensate for the lost hours of sleep. Even when things were going well, after a few consecutive days of riding, my legs ached, my heart pounded, my hands were numb. On the bad days, as I awoke from a two hour nap unable to move, I began to fear that I would never be able to complete the ride, and that I was doing some irreparable damage to my body.

If all of this riding had taken over my life, it also had a big impact on Ann's life as well. Everything we did had to be organized around the fact that I needed to get my miles in. If we were going to babysit the grandkids, somehow I had to at least get an hour or two on the bike. If we had dinner plans, the riding, and my exhaustion had to be taken into account. A visit to Brooklyn to see my mother-in-law had to be done either after my ride or during the visit. The latter option meant I escaped my mother-in-law's cramped New York apartment for a few hours. We had planned two trips that summer. The first was a professional meeting for me. Or as I liked to say, my first history conference as a "has-been," since I had now crossed the great divide from employed to emeritus professor. Between panels I escaped to the gym for an hour on a stationary bike, allowing me to enter 15 miles in my riding log. The second trip was to Oregon for 10 days. I again tried to get to the gym, but since we were driving across the state, and were also babysitting grandkids while my son and his wife attended a wedding, my only riding was a five mile bike tour of Portland and two stints on stationary bikes. Still, it was another 30 miles in the log.

Ann long ago identified what she called the three "As" of academia. Each A represented a special not too flattering characteristic of the typical academic: anal, arrogant, and as-shole. She knew what she was talking about. After all she is married to an academic and had met plenty of others. Ann did not intend her three "As" as a compliment. I jokingly em-braced the first two and would often tell graduate students their value. To be a successful historian, I would pontificate, you needed to be anal. You need to be capable of sitting for 10-12 hours a day in a library reading material which in of itself might not be all that interesting, but when pieced to-gether with years of research, allowed the scholar to draw conclusions and write the books necessary for tenure and promotion. Second, you had to be arrogant. You had to have confidence that the way you saw the sources, the way you explained the past, was correct and that other readings were wrong. However, as important as these two characteristics were, I cautioned would-be historians to guard about pushing either characteristic too far to avoid inevitably becoming an asshole.

I was now using the first two "As" in my training to push myself. Only my anality kept me glued to that bike saddle when my butt was sore, kept my hands gripped to the handlebar when they went numb, and kept my aching legs pedaling mile after mile. Only my arrogance kept me going day after day, asserting that this sixty-seven-year-old could do this trip, even if most people my age are more content with less ambitious goals. In the process I had to avoid taking either characteristic too far. I did not want to become too much of an asshole.

I came to realize that I might be crossing that boundary every time I met people and they asked what I was doing. Since I was doing little else other than preparing for the bike ride, and since it had taken over my life, I inevitably started to tell people about the ride, comparing it to my earlier journey fifty years before and telling them about this book I was writing. I often found myself going into lecture mode, a fault typical of professors. Ann, who had heard my stories all too often, started to get sick of listening to the same thing over and over again. She occasionally sought to guide the conversation away from me to another subject. By mid August, when someone asked if we had any trips planned now that we were both retired, she would simply respond that we would be traveling for a week in upstate New York at the end of the month. She would not mention the bike ride. I got the message and did not add, as I would have earlier in the summer, that the trip was all about me and my ride to Montreal.

Clearly, Ann wished I had never come up with the idea. She also felt left behind. I was the one chiseling my body into a riding machine (now there is an exaggerated and arrogant statement on my part). I was the one around whom our lives revolved. She would rather the two of us do things together. She would rather we move on with our lives as a retired couple.

She was also worried. Repeatedly she told me that she hoped that this would not be the last thing I did. She did not want to be a widow and was afraid my heart would not support the effort. Her ninety-one-year-old mother was no help. She, too, was worried about my heart. She lectured Ann, telling her that my parents had weak hearts and that it was too hot to ride, and the distance was too great. When Ann protested that I would be careful, her mother pulled out one of the oldest clichés in the book: "Just remember if anything happens to Paul, I told you he should not go on this trip." For several weeks in June and early July she called Ann every day checking to see if I had returned from my morning ride. Fortunately for us, her mind soon drifted to other topics and when she did think of it, she came to accept the idea that I was doing this ride whatever my mother-in-law said.

Despite Ann's own concerns, and her own feelings of being left behind, Ann exhibited incredible patience and ultimately supported me in my bicycle endeavor. In fact, she often wanted me to train even harder. If I was going to do the ride, she reasoned, I had best get myself in as good shape as possible to insure that my heart did survive the ordeal. And, perhaps, she hoped, that as I strained my body, and as my bones ached, I might recognize the insanity of the trip. Whatever the reason, it was Ann who encouraged me to increase my miles in July. If I did 35 miles one day, she would urge me to do 45 the next to make sure I could do back-to-back longer rides. About once a week, when the weather was cooperating, she would join me on some of the ride. Either I would do the first part of the day's journey solo, or I would return to the city alone while she drove the car home. This way we would do 20 miles or so together. To mark the event as special, we would have a big lunch in a nice restaurant along the way.

In May I was excited when I managed to do a 20 mile

ride. By mid June I was riding 20 and 30 miles easily. By the end of the month I achieved what the British had failed to do during the Revolutionary War, I had managed to get to Valley Forge and back. In May I logged 168.6 miles. In June I doubled that number. In July I almost doubled it again, for over 550 miles. By the beginning of August, I had ridden more than 1000 miles and almost felt that I was ready for the trip. Before David and Frances arrived I chalked up another 300 miles in August, despite the travel to Oregon.

I began to wish that I had planned the trip differently. By the time of the ride, I knew I could do 40 or 50 miles a day easily. If I had set that pace as a goal and threw in a day of rest now and then, 400 miles would be a snap. As for the time, and the extra expense for the hotels, that would not be a problem. I was retired and had plenty of time on my hands. Although I was not rich, I had more than enough money to splurge on a few extra nights in a Hampton Inn. Had I been doing the ride alone, which Ann said she did not want me to do, or if my co-rider was as old a geezer as I and retired, or if I had agreed on biking during the regular summer break, I could have made a change in plans. But my anal concern with mimicking the 1968 journey had led me to insist on taking only six days and using the same week of the year. Having convinced David to miss the second week of classes to join me, there was no way I could extend the time frame. I was locked in to the six days, and that was that. It was going to be 67 miles a day whether I liked it or not.

I thought all of this through while riding my bike. One of the things you learn when you run long distances, or ride long distances, is that you have plenty of time to think. I spent my entire career at the University of Oklahoma running most days at noon. Usually, I would run with other people, like Rob and David. We would talk, tease each other, and settle the world's problems. I remember one time, when our families were young and our home life consumed with our children, Rob turned to me on a run and laughingly commented that he spent almost more time talking with me on our runs (and in the locker room before and after) than he did with his wife. Occasionally, Rob, or another running partner had to skip a day. When you get into the regular habit of exercising, and are anal enough, you show up at the locker room every day regardless of what others do. That regularity meant that at times I ran by myself. Fine with me. On such runs I would argue with myself, insuring a win in any debate. I would write books on runs – at least in my head. Most of those books never materialized. I would imagine career moves. I would plan out my life. I would keep a constant commentary on all that I saw. To be successful in this type of exercise, to be the long distance runner or biker, you had to be willing to be alone with your own thoughts.

Bike riding provided the same type of experience, even if you were with others. I remember how alone I felt on my bike in 1968, a sensation exacerbated by the fact that Roger and Denis sat atop of a tandem. Now, it is not easy talking on a tandem since the person in the front has to face forward and cannot always be heard by the person behind. But the person in the back can blab all day and project straight into his partner's ear. On a solo bike, especially on the road, it was difficult to ride next to someone else. You always have to be ready for a car to pass you. Even on a bike trail, it was safest to ride single file to avoid other bike, jogging, and walking traffic. Although I am a social person, riding alone was fine with me in the summer of 2018. I let my thoughts run wild. Because I had just retired and was preparing to redo the 1968 ride, not only did I replay events in my career, but I also dreamt of my youth. I thought about all my missteps, the people I had mistreated, and those who mistreated me. I did not dwell too much on my successes.

Memory is a tricky thing. I have been both blessed and cursed with the ability to see things in my own past almost

as if they were right in front of me. This facility to conjure
the past helped me as a historian. It enabled me to remember
things I read and envision the things I read about. But it also
could almost overpower me when applied to my own youth.
When I think about the bike trip in 1968 I can see stretches
of road in front of me. I see Roger and Denis as seventeen,
and I see myself. The nostalgia is bittersweet since I also know
that the people we were then are long gone. In their place is
a whole lifetime of experiences that have changed each of
us and made us different people. I have talked to Roger and
as much as I hear that seventeen-year-old in his voice, I can
also hear that he has changed. As for Denis, I am not sure if
he is alive or dead. My fiftieth high school reunion is coming
and amid the various news and posts placed on facebook is
a list of some of our classmates who have died. Denis is not
listed among them. But many others who I knew are. Of
course, after fifty years it makes sense that our class has lost
some people. But to see their names, and to see their image
in my memory as seventeen is painful.

As much as I conjure visions of my past. As much as I
remember speeding along the shore, riding with Denis and
Roger, sharing the tandem with Nina in the spring of 1968,
somehow that summer is nearly blank. I remember very little from the two months before the trip to Montreal. This
is ironic, since training in the summer of 2018 took over
my life and occupied nearly every day. I cannot recall how
or even where I trained in the summer before the big trip.
The only thing I can remember was that in late June, Roger
and I biked to my parents' cabin in northwest New Jersey.
I had originally believed that we might have made this trip
in 1969. The more I thought about it, the more I realized
that that chronology did not make sense. I spent the summer
after my senior year in high school working in Brooklyn at
my first real job – a Western Union bicycle messenger – not
in New Jersey. As a historian, I long ago realized that most

people have little to document their lives. I was no exception. The only personal documents I have from that era are some old letters written to me from a girl I had met two summers previously and who then became my pen pal. In one of those letters in July 1968 she complimented me for riding 90 miles in preparation for the trip. That letter, and an email from Roger, clinched it: we rode to New Jersey in 1968.

Although I at first could not recall when we did this ride, I can distinctly remember some of the details of the trip. We biked up to the George Washington Bridge and made our way to Route 23 toward Sussex County. At one point near the end of the ride, we broke off from that highway to use the backroads. I did not have a map with all the local roads and we got lost. We turned around to head to a road I was more sure about, racing downhill. When we got to the bottom, I found I had left Roger in the dust – literally. As I passed him on a turn, my tire clipped his and sent him flying. I never felt a thing. I pedaled back up the hill and found Roger a bit sore, at me and in his bones. We rode the remaining 15 miles more carefully since Roger had sprained his wrist. Having reconstructed this trip, I still cannot remember anything else about the following two months. With my bike in New Jersey, I must have taken some practice rides. If I push my memory hard enough, and squint in my mind's eye, I can almost see myself cycling around the lake or on a country lane passing some farm. The image, however, quickly blurs and I cannot be sure if it is memory or imagination. Some portions of the past are just lost to us.

During the summer of 2018, besides dwelling on the past, I also noted the world around me. On weekdays, at least after I passed the Art Museum, there were not many riders. Near Conshohocken and Norristown, there were times when I could peer along a half-mile straight away and not see a soul. On these weekdays half of the infrequent riders were greybeards – men who were probably retired and had time on their hands like me. We formed a certain fraternity and nodded greetings, though we did not know one another or would never see one another again. We were joined in the same battle against time and age, determined to maintain our fitness in the face of our own mortality. During the week there was also more wildlife on the trail. One drizzly June afternoon on the Manayunk canal trail, I startled a deer in the brush only six feet away. He hopped over a few bushes on a parallel course before bounding across the trail some twelve feet in front of me. On another day I saw a fox a tenth of a mile ahead on an isolated section of the trail on the way to Conshohocken. There were groundhogs, chipmunks, and birds a plenty. Fortunately, I never ran into a skunk.

On weekends the trail became more crowded. There were couples out for pleasure rides and clubs of bicycle enthusiasts sporting the same jerseys, packed together, zipping along at 18 to 20 miles per hour. It was on a weekend I came up with the phrase "bicycle cleavage" to describe the young women who wore shirts that dipped down in front and then leaned forward to reach the curved handlebars on their racers, exposing some décolletage regardless of the flatness of their chests. As David frequently observed on similar sights on runs in Oklahoma: "there is nothing wrong with appreciating the beauties of God's creation!"

When I was running in Oklahoma I preferred to use the same route day after day. Once again my anal fixation came to the fore. By following the same course each day, I always knew where I was on the run, how much further I had to go, and my pace. Simply put, I was comfortable. David gave me grief over my desire to consistently run the same route. That was okay with me. Although he would threaten to head off in a different direction, especially when the regular path faced a stout Oklahoma wind, he always relented and remained by my side.

I fell into the same pattern on most of my training rides,

staying riveted to the Schuylkill River Trail. In my head I divided the route into a series of two to three mile stretches, each with its own special characteristics. The most challenging section was in Manayunk on the streets. I referred to this segment as the "Manayunk Hills." In part because it was a rainy summer, and in part I knew I had to do some hill and road training, in early July I stopped using the trail along the Manayunk Canal, even though it was one of the most enjoyable parts of the ride and was almost totally flat. Instead, I followed Main Street in Manayunk to its end, turned right and headed up a steep short incline on Leverington Avenue and then turned left, across traffic, still going uphill on to Umbria Street. The climb, especially because of the turns and the constant need to negotiate traffic, took my breath away. At first I had to stop at least once to get my heart rate down. I did not want to die on Ann while in training. Eventually I made it to the top of that hill, coasted to the next upgrade and then negotiated a series of hills for about a mile before Umbria meets Shawmut Avenue and a hairpin turn downhill returned me to the paved Schuylkill River Trail. I noticed that even some of the youngsters struggled with these hills. Heading back to Philly was a little easier since the Shawmut-Umbria climb was not as steep and almost brought you to the top of the hill. Also on the return there was one straight steep downhill section where just gliding I hit 32 miles per hour. That was about as fast as I wanted to go on a bike at my age.

I actually learned a few things with all of this biking. When I bought the Trek FXS-5 I traded out the tires for puncture resistant treads. I wanted to avoid having a flat tire. The thicker rubber would not stop a nail, but would discourage less lethal punctures. I soon began to think that my tires were too wide, even though they were not as wide as more traditional hybrids. Rider after rider zipped past me on the trail, especially on the weekends when the young crowd turned out. Of course, as Ann noted, they were passing me because they were thirty to forty years my junior. Regardless, I convinced myself that thinner tires would help. The bike store hipsters had repeated to me that the thinner the tire, the less contact with the road, which meant less resistance and a faster pace. This sounded like real science. So after paying an additional $75 for the puncture resistant tires when I first bought the bike, I upped the ante by paying another $100 (cost plus labor) for thinner tires two months later. I increased my speed marginally, but whether that was because I did not adjust my bike computer (the modern odometer and speedometer) for the smaller diameter of the thin tires, I could not tell. The youngsters continued to zip by me since at most I added a mile per hour to my speed. I also came to see the utility of bike shoes that clipped onto the pedals. At a rest stop I overheard some middle age male riders, whose oversized bellies and butts should never have been squished into spandex, proclaiming the advantages of clip-ons. Again, there was science here. Clip-ons propel the bike forward with both the downward and upward motion of your legs. I, however, could not find any bike shoe wide enough for my 6E feet. Rather than cramming my web-like feet into a narrower shoe, or try shoes two sizes too large, I decided to forego this investment. In addition, I accidentally discovered the advantage of drafting. I knew that bike racers drafted all the time. I watched one race on television that summer in which the announcers described how several teammates would ride in front of the sprinter to form a wind break to save that sprinter's energy for the final leg of the race. I understood how it worked, but I did not think that drafting would have a big impact on my pathetic pace. Since I was riding alone in training, there was little opportunity to try out the practice. Either other riders zipped past me, or I slogged past the real laggards. In either case, the disparities in our speed prevented any drafting. One day late in July, I was near Norristown moving at a decent speed, when I heard a small group of riders following me. Were they drafting behind me? I wasn't sure. I must have relaxed a little and slowed a tad. They passed me, but did not pull away and leave me in the dust. The group consisted of two women and a man, all in their mid-thirties. Before I realized it, I was tucked in about six feet behind the two women who were riding next to each other chatting away. I was doing about 12 to 13 miles per hour when they passed. For the next four or five miles, until we got to Valley Forge, I remained tucked behind these two, going 15 to 16 miles per hour. It was so easy that I was even able to stop pedaling for five to ten seconds at a time without losing momentum. Of course, it just worked out that the women were wearing spandex. Yet it was not their attire that kept me going. It was the pace.

* * *

All throughout the summer David and I maintained a near constant stream of emails, informing each other of our progress in training. We both had ups and downs. Every time I expressed a concern that I might not be able to do the ride, David was there to reassure me. He was a true cheerleader. However encouraging he might be, he was too competitive not to remind me of his edge in riding experience and miles. When I told him that I had crossed the 1000 mile threshold, he responded that he had done 1200 miles in the same time frame and 2400 miles since January. I forgave him this vanity. David, after all, was logging these miles in Oklahoma in the summertime and rather than riding only in the morning to avoid heat like me, he was often riding in the evening when the temperatures usually were their hottest. He also experienced his own trials. David had two international trips that summer. His travel to Germany was harmless enough and occurred after he journeyed to Bolivia. The South American trip was a part of David's endeavor to save the world by providing clean water to the nether regions of the earth.

He visited a remote Andean village which had benefitted from a water project he had worked on. The locals provided a great fiesta for David and his co-workers, offering them coca leaves to chew (I was surprised that David indulged) and a huge feast. David admitted later that he was leery of eating this food, but as with the coca leaves, he felt obliged to partake, regardless of the possible effects. This experience, as he explained, was a scene right out of National Geographic and was one of the highlights of his career. It also struck him a low blow. He picked up an intestinal bug that not only sent him running to the toilet, but knocked him off his feet – he passed out! When David fell, he tweaked his knee. For a week or two, I anxiously awaited his updates as he worked his stomach and knee back into shape. I was glad that David was trying to save the world. I still selfishly hoped that his good intentions would not wreck my bike ride.

I had my own less serious medical mishaps. A week and a half before the beginning of the Montreal trip, as I was busy trying to rebuild my stamina after the visit to Oregon, I developed a problem. We had returned on August 8 and I took the ninth off to recover from the red eye flight. On the tenth, our wedding anniversary, I did 30 miles. On the twelfth I rode 45.6 miles to Valley Forge and back. On the fourteenth I repeated the distance. Then, when it got good and hot, on the fifteenth I rode 53.6 miles. Not only did I do the now usual Valley Forge route, but I toured the whole national historic park. It added miles and provided an opportunity to do some hills. There is even a section on a regular road with automobile traffic which I thought would be useful. Most of my biking had been on trails; most of the Montreal route would be on roads with cars to deal with. I loved the ride. There is a wonderfully tranquil character to Valley Forge with its recreated soldiers' huts, old cannon on the hillsides, and open countryside. It was the middle of the week and there were just a handful of older women and stay-at-home moms out walking. There were almost no tourists and no other bikers. I found the twisting and turning, as well as the uphill and downhill, peaceful and relaxing.

Of course Valley Forge was anything but tranquil in the winter of 1777-78. George Washington's disordered army was full of desertion and discontent. The men smelled, were poorly clothed and were hungry. According to the textbooks, out of this experience Washington and Baron Van Steuben forged (get it) a powerful fighting force. Yet the war continued to rage for six more years. While I pedaled so easily along the Schuylkill, I could not help but wonder why the British never attempted to traverse the twenty odd miles and attack an army that was already beginning to disintegrate. The mythology holds that the British were merely following the practice of eighteenth-century armies by not fighting in the cold and snow. But when Washington broke those rules in his surprise attack on the Hessians at Trenton on December 26, 1776, Lord Cornwallis led a British army across New Jersey to trap Washington between Trenton and the Delaware River on January, 2, 1777. Washington only managed to escape by keeping his campfires burning and slipping to the south and east. Perhaps, then, it was the ability of Washington to retreat – something he did repeatedly in 1776 and 1777 – that convinced the British not to bother with marching to Valley Forge. Besides, they had captured the largest and most important city in the United States and many of the locals were signing loyalty oaths to King George. The rebellion was about to implode on its own. Lord Howe could remain ensconced in Philadelphia and await the disintegration of the Continental Army, or have his replacement deliver the coup de grace in the summer.

After I completed the eight mile circuit of the national park, and as I replayed the events of the winter of 1777-78 at Valley Forge in my head, I discovered another reason why this trek could be fraught with difficulties – the wear and tear on the body. With approximately ten miles left on my return ride, I began to develop a hotspot on my butt. Note, I did not develop a hot butt; only a hot spot on my butt. I immediately recognized that this could be serious. I managed to get home without too much damage. That night, Ann did some research. I had already come to the conclusion that the irritation had developed from sweat saturating my underwear, causing the seams of my briefs to rub on my butt. As I lay in bed that night drifting blissfully into sleep and glad I was not sitting on a bicycle, Ann was reading on the internet all about butt ointments for bike riders. Of course, my problem was not unique. There was a whole constellation of products for sores where the sun don't shine: Chamois Butt'r, Petal Power Joy Ride Creme; Gooch Guard Chamois Cream; Assos Chamois Creme. The bottom line was that I needed to get some of this creme, and get it soon.

The solution to my saddle soreness was more than skin deep. I also needed to make an adjustment to my cycling attire. Knowing that David had thousands of bike miles under his butt, and knowing he had special quick drying underwear he wore when he traveled to exotic locales, I had asked David a month earlier what he wore under his bike pants. To my surprise, he replied "nothing." I was appalled and believed that maybe David had spent too much time in underdeveloped countries and had lost a notch or two on his standards of personal hygiene. As David should have explained, bike pants were designed to be worn without underwear. Indeed, as I discovered upon googling the question, there were even antibacterial agents in the padding of some bike pants. As one website informed me, I had diagnosed my seamly problem correctly. The bike pants padding avoided the rubbing since they were designed to cling to my body, absorb sweat, and prevent chafing. I also learned that the pants should be washed after each use. I had simply dried them out overnight and plopped them back on again. Maybe it was my personal

hygiene that was lacking. Chamois cream enhanced the protection offered by the pants and provided a further antimi-
crobial guard. At this time I also decided to ditch the shorts
over the bike pants despite my flabbiness. The shorts turned
out to be cumbersome on long rides and wearing one less
layer made sense in the heat of the summer. Having gained
an education in bike wear, I took the next day off, ordered
two more bike pants for the ride, bought some chamois
creme (I now knew exactly where to apply it) and prepared
to go Commando! When I told David about my revelations,
he simply replied, "Commando indeed. And like you ever
listen to me." This response launched a series of exchanges,
playing off the name of his preferred butt creme. I wrote to
him "I should have known you knew butt'r than me." David
answered in kind: "butt'r late than never" to which I said "no
butt about it." After years of running together, these two old
professors could be pretty silly sometimes.

No sooner had my butt healed, then I caught a summer
cold from my two-year-old grandson who was learning how
to share after all. I awoke that Saturday, eight days before
the scheduled departure from Brooklyn, and after having not
biked for two days, determined to ride at least to Falls Bridge
and back for an easy 12 miles. It was drizzling and humid,
my nose was stuffy, my throat was sore, and my bones ached.
The cold, which had been coming on for two days had struck
with a vengeance. I would not ride that day. As miserable
as I felt, I thanked my lucky stars that the cold hit me that
weekend and not the following weekend, when the ride was
to begin. I also decided that with 1200 miles under my belt,
missing a few more days of riding would not matter.

Chapter 7

On the Brink

THE WEEK BEFORE the big ride flew by. I was still recovering from my cold, but I decided that I had best get
some miles in anyway. On Monday and Thursday I biked
to Falls Bridge and back with Ann. On Tuesday I managed
thirty miles by myself. So before David and Frances arrived,
I had added about 55 miles to my total. It was not the 100
plus I had hoped for. Nor had I managed to cycle for the
67 miles in one day that was the planned average on our
way to Montreal. Between the cold and getting ready for
the arrival of our guests, I did not have the time nor did I
have the strength. Getting those extra miles in, I concluded,
would not make that much difference and why use up energy I would need the next week. The last thing I wanted to
do was to begin the ride tired. In short, it was too late to do
extra miles. That ride should have been completed the week
before. But then I was struggling with a sore butt and a serious summer cold.

Among the other tasks I had to complete that week, was
picking up David's bike which he had shipped to the shop
where I had bought my bike. When I arrived at the shop,
Ray was there. As was Gregg, the main contact person David had used in making his arrangements. Neither Ray nor
I mentioned the beers and the promised bike repair training
session. Ray and Gregg were all excited about my upcoming
ride and were impressed with my 1200 miles of training. I

admitted that I should have worked more on hills, but both thought that with that number of miles under my belt in just three months, I would be ready for the trip. I paid the $100 fee they charged for unpacking the bike and tuning it up now and then re-packing and shipping the bike when we returned. I intended to collect the money later from David, but Ann convinced me to tell David that I would spring for the money since he had airline tickets and the shipping fee from Norman to cover. These were expenses I did not have. I left the bike shop pumped, knowing that both Ray and Gregg were rooting me on.

In the meantime, Ann was getting a little nervous about the whole trip – and not just about my riding a bicycle. Although she had known Frances for almost as long as I had known David, they had only interacted occasionally. We had gone to each other's houses for dinner or parties a few times. Ann and Frances had never really spent much time together, and certainly no time one on one. Now, she was going to have to be with Frances for six days in a row. Yes, it would be an opportunity to get to know one another, but what if things did not work out between them. They came from different worlds. Ann was a New Yorker – a tried and true Yankee – whose political opinions were decidedly liberal. Frances was a Southerner through and through who was more conservative in her politics. Ann had taught in public schools for thirty years before retiring. Frances was a stay at home mom who had home schooled her children for several years. Ann was a high-church Lutheran. Frances was a low church evangelical. Ann was a high energy person who liked to be busy all the time. Frances took things slower and was content to spend much of her vacations lying around reading a book. There was reason for concern.

As it worked out, they developed a great fondness for each other. When David and Frances arrived in Philadelphia that Friday, Frances announced that although she had originally opposed the idea of David joining me because she was concerned with his riding on roads packed with all those Yankees, she had decided that it was an opportunity David could not turn down. Besides, she asserted, she planned on making a new good friend – Ann. She told Ann to go ahead and plan their itinerary and she would do whatever Ann decided they should do. Ann was still a little nervous, but over the next week she poured over guide books and selected the historic sites and mansions that the two of them greatly enjoyed together. Ann and I are a few years older than David and Frances, and our children were a few years older than their children. We already have a couple of grandchildren. Frances and David were expecting their first grandchild. So Ann could dispense all kinds of advice to Frances about being a grandmother. The two of them also were interested in genealogy and discussed family history. Despite their conservatism, neither Frances nor David were fans of the current president. And, both Frances and Ann enjoyed having a glass of wine in the evening.

I should also make one more comment about Ann: not only is she a careful planner, she is almost always right. Sometimes it takes me a little while to recognize that she is right. Sometimes that little while can last years, other times a few days. Mostly, I recognize that she is right immediately and do whatever she tells me. As a part of her careful planning she turned to me early in that last week and suggested I contact our insurance agent to make sure our car insurance would cover us in Canada. I dismissed this suggestion as a little over the top and thought Ann was worrying about a problem that just did not exist. Yes, having moved we had a new insurance policy, but of course, it had to cover us when we traveled north of the border. On Friday morning I decided that before she reminded me again I would check on the car insurance. I shot our new insurance agent a quick email. I expected an easy answer that I hoped would alleviate Ann's concerns. Well, Ann was right and I should have taken care of this chore earlier. My email read: "I wanted to check and make sure there will be no insurance issues if I drive to Canada. I am assuming that there will not be. Is that correct?" Within the hour, the insurance agent responded: "Actually we will need to do an endorsement. When are you going, when will you be returning, will you be the only one driving your vehicle?"

Now we had a problem. Emails went frantically back and forth. We even called the insurance agent to make sure we understood exactly what he meant by an endorsement. Apparently, Canada, which was then in the midst of tense trade negotiations and in a testy relationship with Donald Trump, was stopping some American drivers at the border and insisting that they carry a special document printed on Canadian paper demonstrating that they were covered by car insurance. Our agent told us not to worry. We were covered by our insurance and our insurance company would mail us the document in an overnight envelope. Great, we thought, all we had to do is delay our departure for Brooklyn on Saturday until after the document arrived since all of these exchanges took place early in the business day on Friday.

Of course it was not that simple. Our agent is a broker for multiple companies so the endorsement was not coming from him. We were therefore dealing with second hand information. We also realized that since it was Friday, the beginning of the weekend, "overnight" might not be a true overnight. In the meantime we had picked up David and Frances at the airport. The four of us discussed the situation over and over again. David and I said there was nothing to worry about. Our wives remained worried. By Saturday morning Ann wanted me to call the insurance company directly. With almost no hesitation I did so. I had learned my lesson. If I had contacted the insurance agent the previous Monday, when she first asked me, we would have had the endorsement in hand. Well, it turned out that the company had sent the letter, but that there was no guarantee it would get there on the weekend. I asked if the company could send the endorsement to one of the hotels we knew we would be staying at. Maybe, but that would have to be a decision made by a supervisor during the regular business week. In other words, we needed to wait until Monday for an answer. "What about driving to an office of the company to pick up the endorsement?" That, too, might be a possibility, but again the decision would have to be made by a supervisor. Besides, the only office in the region that issued the endorsements was in Glens Falls, New York. "Great," I said, "we will be passing right through Glens Falls." Imagining the whole trip into Canada crumbling before my eyes, I then asked "What happens if we fail to get an endorsement." Well, it turns out that it was possible to purchase separate insurance at some border crossings to cover the days you were in Canada. Great, I thought, we have options. The endorsement did not arrive that Saturday.

Ultimately we pursued yet another option. My son called and when he heard of our predicament, he offered to check our mail on Monday. To do so he had to wait until his young children were asleep and then drive from the suburbs to central Philadelphia. He then went immediately to a 24-hour Fed Ex office and expressed the endorsement to one of the hotels where we would be staying. To our great relief, we received this package on Wednesday evening. As it turned out, all of this worrying was much ado about nothing. When Ann and Frances crossed into Canada a week later, the border control never asked to see any proof of insurance.

David and I had planned to go for a short ride that Friday evening in Philadelphia. I wanted to show him the Schuylkill bike path, explain to him about bicycle cleavage, and make sure that his bike had been properly put together and tuned. With all of the excitement of their arrival Friday

afternoon, a trip to Target, and discussion about the insurance endorsement, we decided to put the ride off until Saturday morning. We had to wait to leave until the late after-

noon mail arrived
anyway. David enjoyed
the ride and was im-
pressed with all of the
sights along the trail.
He was especially
pleased when we brief-
ly stopped at the Falls
Bridge before turning
around. A couple of
twenty-somethings on
their own bikes com-
mented on how sleek and beautiful his celeste (a mixture of
sky blue and pale green) Bianchi looked. David simply
glowed. I glowered since no one noticed my Trek FXS-5
which was almost as expensive as David's Bianchi. Maybe I
should have bought that Specialized bike that Ryan had said
would make heads turn.

After the mail arrived with no endorsement, we headed
for Brooklyn and the Gregory Hotel – the only real hotel in
Bay Ridge. We gave David and Frances a brief tour of our
old neighborhood, driving past our childhood homes, our
high school, and the home of Frank Reagan of *Blue Bloods*.
We then took David and Frances to our favorite pizza parlor
for real Brooklyn style pizza. That night as I lay down to
sleep I almost could not believe it. The bike ride was really
going to happen. I was on the brink of a great adventure. It
all seemed so unreal.

Part Two

The Rides

Chapter 8

Day One

WE BEGAN BOTH rides full of excitement and optimism. Whatever lay ahead of us, we were ready – or so we thought. In 1968 we started later than we intended. We had spent the night before at my parents' house while they were away at their cabin in New Jersey. There was no wild teenage party. No beer. No girls. Just three seventeen-year-olds staying up later than they should watching old movies on TV. There was also no wild party the night before the 2018 trip, although there were girls in our rooms – our wives. Older and wiser, we did not stay up very late despite our excitement. We simply went to sleep eager for an early start the next morning. We aimed to leave at 7:30 from the Hotel Gregory, less than a half mile from my childhood home. It was nearly eight before we pushed off amid pictures and well wishes from our wives. In 1968 we posed briefly for an old fashioned "selfie" that Denis took on a timer with his camera balanced on a parked car in front of my house. Unfortunately, this is the only picture I have from the 1968 trip and it is of poor quality since it is copied from my high school student newspaper and accompanied an article Roger wrote of our adventure. Not shown in the picture was Roger's guitar, which he wore strapped to his back, nor how I had attached my pack to my bike. In an effort to maintain the symmetry between the two rides, David and I made a small detour at my old block where we posed for pictures in front of what was once my parents' house and the start point of the 1968 ride. We did not quite capture the same angle. David snapped one shot of only me right in front of the house, and another modern "selfie" of the two of us.

This brief stop also allowed us to follow the exact same route for both rides, at least for the first three or four miles. In 1968 and 2018, we headed from my old house the wrong way on a one way street to Fourth Avenue and then followed that thoroughfare toward "downtown" Brooklyn. In 1968 we aimed straight for the Brooklyn Bridge, turning off Fourth Avenue on Flatbush Avenue and then connecting to a street that took us under the bridge where we could access the walkway by climbing a flight of stairs. In 1968 there was no other legal way to get on the bridge as a pedestrian or on a bike.

When I was seventeen, I did not give a second thought to riding in the city streets. All three of us had spent countless miles working our way through red lights, and developing almost a sixth sense in reading what the motorized traffic might be doing. And, of course, we were young and assumed we were invincible. Fifty years later, I had lost some of my edge and knew all too well how vulnerable I was while biking in the street. The profusion of red lights therefore slowed our pace. As much experience on a bike as David had, he had not ridden in such an urban environment, watching for doors opening from parked cars, looking out for potholes, peering into side streets to determine if traffic was speeding down at you, swerving around double-parked vehicles, and even sizing up the pedestrians along the way to see if they posed any threat.

Physically, this first part of our journey had changed little in fifty years. The pavement was still a deep black asphalt typical of New York streets. Most of the buildings had been built in the early twentieth century and already seemed old in 1968. A few had been torn down by 2018. There used to be a beautiful stone Methodist Church dating from 1899, with a magnificent stained glass window and clock tower on the corner of Ovington Ave. There now stands a new public school – with some of its facade covered in stone similar to the torn down church and a small clock tower. Other than a

few such alterations, nothing much had changed until about
Twentieth Street. Here, in what had once been a marginal
neighborhood, new fancy apartment houses are sprouting
everywhere. To give David a better sense of this urban development, I decided to make the first of many deviations from
the 1968 route. The fastest way to get to Brooklyn Bridge on
a bike would have been to ride exactly the same way we did
in 1968. Instead, at Third Street we made a left. I wanted to
show David the new Whole Foods on the corner of Third
Avenue – or, as the Brooklyn comics used to say - "da kohna
of terd and terd." When I was growing up, a warehouse stood
on this corner in the middle of an industrial zone with run-
down buildings and junk yards all around. Now, the area was
packed with hipsters and thirty-somethings. Not only were
there new buildings on Fourth Avenue, but they were also
cropping up all throughout this neighborhood. Even the
Gowanus Canal sported luxury apartment houses which
promised either views of Manhattan, or of a park and the canal itself – almost as if this once pathetic and polluted body
of water was akin to the Grand Canal in Venice. As we approached Third Avenue I could see the draw bridge raising
over the canal. To avoid further delay, we made a right turn
on Third Avenue and went to Bergen Street, down Bergen
Street past a slew of brownstones, which I told David was an
iconic form of housing in Brooklyn that usually had elabo-
rately wood-paneled rooms inside. We made our way to the
waterfront. Again we could see an urban transformation.
What had once been a series of docks inaccessible to the
general public, and the haunt of longshoreman right out of
the movie *On the Waterfront*, now stood a lovely park with
twisting walking and riding trails, populated by fashionable
women walking their foofoo dogs. The old piers had been
re-purposed into tennis and basketball courts. We took this
detour so I could show David the skyline of lower Manhattan. Of course we stopped for pictures. At the base of the

Brooklyn Bridge, we headed uphill to find an entrance to the walkway. It had been awhile since I ridden to the bridge and I had to feel my way toward the old staircase. Although it is now possible to ride straight onto the bridge from a bike lane on the street, I opted for the stairs. They were an important reminder of my 1968 journey.

The iconic Brooklyn Bridge, too, has undergone a transformation over the last fifty years. The bridge itself, although it has had many face lifts, remains essentially the same. Ever since it was completed in 1883, it has stood as a monumental achievement and an architectural masterpiece. In 1968, few pedestrians or cyclists used the Brooklyn Bridge. Since then, it has become a destination for tourists. When I crossed the bridge when I was seventeen there were signs prohibiting all photography because the bridge afforded a great view of the Brooklyn Navy Yard. Even then these signs were outdated since they were holdovers from the Second World War when the activity at the navy yard was a military secret. Those signs have now long ago been taken down. In 2018, I hoped

to make it to the bridge before the big crowds. I was afraid that on a Sunday in the summer there would be so many people on the bridge that we would have to walk our bikes across. Fortunately, although there were already plenty of tourists and others, we did not have to dismount. We chose to anyhow. Practically everyone stopped for pictures, including us. The bridge is just too magnificent, and the skyline too prominent, not to seize a "selfie" moment. It was hard to imagine that using a camera on the Brooklyn Bridge was once illegal. We stopped near one young man with a fancy camera taking pictures of his girlfriend, although she well could have been a model. I snapped a photo of David on my phone, making sure the young woman was in the background. I couldn't resist the impish impulse to have straight-laced David sharing the picture with such a young and attractive woman, and intended to send it to our running buddies back in Oklahoma. When I did so later that day, they understood immediately and jokingly commented on it. David asked the young man to take a snapshot of the two of us. The result was probably the best picture taken during the entire trip. The guy knew how to frame a photo.

Not only was it difficult to access the bridge from Brooklyn in 1968, but in Manhattan the only way to exit the walkway was through a subway station, which meant you had to walk down one set of stairs and up another. No subway entrance for us in 2018. We rode off the bridge onto a designated bike path on the city street. As far as I remember, there were no bike lanes in 1968. Cyclists simply had to claim their little piece of the road off to the side and hope that nothing bigger, either car, truck, or bus, contested it. Likewise, there were only a handful of true bike paths in New York City in the sixties. Now, they are spread throughout all five boroughs. With few alternatives, and really without much thought, in 1968 we headed uptown on the streets, intending to hook up with Broadway north of Columbus Circle. Although it was Sunday morning, with little real traffic, even then we understood it might not be a good idea to ride up Broadway, which was one way going downtown, until we could go with the traffic after Columbus Circle, when it became a two way street. Many New Yorkers may not realize it, but Broadway, perhaps the most famous avenue in the world, was originally a major conduit for exiting the city. Unlike most streets in Manhattan which meet at right angles, it heads diagonally north and west, continuing into the Bronx. Broadway also is technically part of the national highway system: it is the same US 9 that runs along the east side of the Hudson River, then extends north all the way to the Canadian border. In a manner of speaking, although on both trips we left this high-way at times, US 9 remained our compass needle that kept us headed in the right direction. We might deviate from it, but sooner or later we returned to it. I should add that in 2018 there is a state bikeway with the number 9 that sometimes was located on the shoulder of US 9, and at other times fol-lowed different routes.

As a matter of safety, in 2018 we did not follow the 1968 route through Manhattan. I also thought we might minimize some of the hills in northern Manhattan by riding along the Hudson. I remembered one stretch of Broadway from 122nd Street to 135th Street where the terrain dips and the subway briefly runs above ground, before another uphill covers it. I was less concerned with another possible problem. Roger says that when we were near Harlem some boys threw eggs at us. I have only the dimmest memory of that and wonder if it was not on our practice trip to Bear Mountain. Regardless, I thought an "egging" highly unlikely in 2018.

Once we coasted down into Manhattan from the Brook-lyn Bridge, David and I followed the bike lane past Cham-bers Street and onto Reade Street, which then led us to the West Side. This route was not an option in 1968. At that time the Lower West Side was still an active port with busy

wharves separated from the city by the elevated West Side
Highway which had been built in the 1920s. That structure
was rapidly deteriorating in the 1960s and was closed to traffic in 1973. Eventually in the 1980s it was torn down and replaced with a wide boulevard and the creation of a greenway
that included the bike path we took. Again, we were early
enough to beat the big crowds. On a Sunday afternoon in the
summer, the bikeway becomes congested with cyclists, skate-
boarders, skaters, joggers, and a whole range of humanity. We
did have to use my ding-a-ling bell a few times, but we were
also able to ride next to one another and maintain at least a
twelve mile per hour pace for most of the way. We enjoyed
wonderful views of what remained of the once active seaport,
including multiple piers that housed parking lots, driving
ranges, tennis courts, shops, restaurants, and a host of other
attractions. As we continued up the river, I tried to imagine
what it looked like in the 1960s. I remember as a child getting a thrill when my father would drive the family along the
West Side Highway and we would look to see if the ocean
liner my father had taken from Norway in 1936 was in port.
I learned many years later that this same vessel had brought
Ann's parents to the United States in 1951. The *Stavangerfjord* struck me as a magnificent ship and I always thought it
would have been grand to have sailed across the Atlantic in
it. Launched in 1917, it was scrapped in 1964, a casualty to
jet airplane travel. When I searched for images of this ship,
there was one picture from its last days that made the vessel
look more like a tramp steamer than an ocean liner. Today,
along the Hudson, there are not many ships of any kind.
However, the Intrepid Air and Space Museum is housed in
a retired aircraft carrier, the USS *Intrepid*, that impressively
looms above anyone on the bike trail. Oddly, dwarfing what
was once considered one of the largest ships to sail the seas,
was a modern cruise ship docked nearby. Both make the old
steamships like the *Stavangerfjord* look like bathtub toys.

David and I biked along the Hudson until we reached the Little Red Lighthouse under the George Washington Bridge, a landmark I remembered from my youth. He was impressed with the size and scope of the Hudson as we headed uptown. I informed him that the river was almost a mile wide and deep enough to handle any vessel in the world. It was a far cry from the South Canadian River that runs near Norman, Oklahoma. That waterway was often little more than a trickle and can usually be crossed on foot – except when it rains and becomes a raging torrent of mile-wide rapids. We took a few more photos and had a brief snack. I thought things were going just great. We were making good time and I had plenty of energy left.

After this brief rest stop, David and I ran into our first hiccup of the trip. Just past the George Washington Bridge the bike trail was impassable. A sign said that the bridge over the railway tracks and highway was closed for inspection. In the distance we could see another fence and noticed two young men lift their bikes over this eye-high impediment, and continue on. At seventeen I might have tried the same maneuver. At sixty-seven and sixty we turned around, and coasted downhill. We backtracked a half mile to another footbridge off the bike path, stopping briefly at a port-o-potty nearby. Neither of us had used the toilet since leaving the hotel. I had no real inclination to pee, a fact that should have warned me that I was not hydrating enough. With my aging bladder I ordinarily relieve myself every hour or so. The detour forced us into the streets and into Washington Heights – meaning we now had to climb several hills. I knew exactly where we were, but was unsure of how to get from our location to Broadway and across the Harlem River. I spared David the mini lecture on the Battle of Fort Washington when the American forces entrenched on this high ground were overwhelmed by a British assault on three sides. On that sad day in November 1776, almost three thousand Continental soldiers surrendered. As we pedaled uphill, it was clear to me we had not avoided all the hills in northern Manhattan. Before we knew it we found ourselves high above the rest of the city, circling the Cloisters. I could see Broadway a couple hundred feet beneath us. Out came our phones to check the GPS, but this program was not that useful here. We were at one of the highest points in Manhattan and it was unclear from the two dimensional map what street would lead us to the level of the rest of the city. I spied a short staircase down to some walking trails that looked like they might take us to the bottom of the hill. We picked up our bikes, got on the trail and, after several twists and turns, found Broadway. I told David I knew what I was doing all of the time.

Here, we briefly followed in the footsteps – maybe I should say tire tracks – of the 1968 journey. On Broadway, we headed north, past the Dyckman House – an old Dutch farmstead – and across the Harlem River and into the Bronx. Once again we experienced the joys of navigating the streets of New York, watching out for traffic and avoiding getting "doored" by someone leaving a parked car. In the Bronx, we even cycled under an elevated subway.

It was in the Bronx in 1968 that my biggest mishap of the first day occurred. Shortly after entering this northern borough, and what was almost a foreign country to three Brooklyn boys, I discovered that I had not secured my backpack to my seat very well and that it had fallen down and was sitting on the tire. Without my noticing, the tire wore a hole in the bag, which was a daypack that was a relic from my father's days in the army in WW II. The tire was not finished with its dirty work; it then began to rub out a hole in my spare underwear. This situation had to be fixed. We needed to find a fender. Today, we would use our cell phones to look up the nearest store for such a purchase. In 1968 we let "our fingers do the walking" and relied on a phone book at a telephone booth to find a bike shop nearby. I purchased a fender for my pack to rest on and to prevent further harm to my spare clothes. After attaching the fender to the bike, we returned to Broadway and headed north. Although the damage was limited to my supply of tighty whities, the holes in my underpants had serious implications. I decided at first not to use the damaged goods since they had holes and black rubber marks on them. Not changing underwear was a mistake since I ended up with a severe case of jock itch that made pedaling more difficult than it needed to be. Within a few days I went ahead and wore the holey underwear to save my crotch.

Relying on the same logic as we used for Manhattan, David and I planned to leave the 1968 route that would have followed Broadway all the way through the Bronx into Yonkers and beyond. This would be some loss. I vividly remembered crossing into Yonkers from the Bronx and wondering when the city would end. That is, there was no real difference between the northern Bronx and Yonkers. The city went on and on. Roger saw things a little differently. He recalls that the Bronx already seemed like an alien place and that to his Brooklyn sensibilities both the Bronx and Yonkers appeared equally strange. Despite my interest in nostalgically following the original route, I decided upon a safer option. David had already tasted the joys of street riding and had cycled under an elevated subway for a mile. That was enough of an urban adventure. We headed for a bike trail that ran through Van Courtland Park that would connect to the Westchester County Trail. Both paths were examples of the rails to trails movement. All through the United States old railway lines have now been transformed into bikeways. The longest of such trails is in Missouri and stretches 240 miles across the width of the state. The first of such trails opened in 1967 in Wisconsin. There were not many rails to trails in 1968 and they only began to expand rapidly in the 1980s with federal government encouragement. Some rails to trails are paved,

many are crushed stone. Some are dirt. The Van Courtland
Park version was not just dirt but also had plenty of railway
ties still on it. Riding was made difficult by these logs strewn
across the trail. At times the trail became almost impassable
because a recent rain left large sections muddy. Surrounded
by woods, golf courses, and underbrush, we had little choice
but to plow on. Once we crossed into Westchester, however,
the path became paved. Although parts of it were bumpy
from expanding tree roots, overall this Westchester section
of the path was wonderful. There were a few other riders on
the trail, but for most of the way, we could ride side by side,
just chatting away like we did when we went running for all
those years. Google Maps had wanted us to stay on this bikeway all the way to Mahopac and then take a regular highway
north and east to Fishkill where we had hotel reservations.
This route would have been longer and hillier than the one
we followed.

We left the bike trail at Elmsforth, about 18 miles north
of the Bronx-Westchester line and before it veered too far
from the Hudson River and US 9. I wanted to ride the 1968
route the rest of the day. I had remembered Tarrytown as
being a particularly attractive place and I wanted to bike
through Washington Irving territory. For my entire teaching career, I had students in my American Revolution class
read Irving's short story "Rip Van Winkle." This supposed
children's tale, in which a ne'er-do-well Rip goes into the
Catskill Mountains and falls asleep for twenty years, cap-
tures many of the great social and political changes that had
occurred during the Revolution. I also could not resist taking
David through Sleepy Hollow, the supposed location of Irving's tale about the Headless Horseman. Even when I was
in high school I was familiar with Irving's stories and excited
about passing through this part of the Hudson Valley.

It was at this point that I ran into serious problems. In
2018 my underwear was not involved in my troubles, because, after all, I did not wear any. Instead, I began to con-

front my physical limitations as a sixty-seven-year-old who had not been hydrating enough. We hit a series of hills that sent my heart pounding. I initially only had to stop to get my heart rate down. I had used this method of dealing with hills on a number of my early training rides in Manayunk. Once we passed Tarrytown and headed into Sleepy Hollow, I knew I was getting into trouble. I did not see a Headless Horseman. But I might as well have. On one hill in front of the cemetery where Washington Irving is buried, I needed to stop, get off the bike and lean against a stone wall in front of the tombstones to take a breather. After I dismounted my bike, removed my helmet and skull cap (worn to protect against the sun on my bald head), the world began to spin and get blurry. I was afraid I was going to pass out. This was serious trouble. I could also feel my heart thumping in my chest. I had to lay down and raise my legs higher than my head. This reconfiguration of my body would get blood flowing to my brain and hopefully stave off hallucinations and unconsciousness. For-

tunately, we were on a hill, so I could lay down on the grass with my head toward the bottom of the hill and my feet elevated. I was obviously suffering from the heat. Even though it was only 82 degrees, I had become dehydrated. So I lay there drinking water and eating a protein bar. David, who had thousands of miles of experience in the heat, had almost finished both of his water bottles. I had only drunk about half a water bottle. After a few minutes, the leaves and tree branches above me began to come into focus. Great, I got up. I leaned against the stone wall. Oops, the world started to spin again. I had to go down three times, fortunately not for a final count, before I was strong enough to proceed. The whole ordeal probably took about forty minutes.

In 1968 we had negotiated these hills with hardly a problem. Not so in 2018. In 1968 we had walked up only one hill the entire trip – on Day Five at Three Mile Mountain near Lake George. After feeling strong enough to continue, I now began to walk up this hill in Sleepy Hollow. And for the rest of that day, and indeed every day of the journey, I walked the hills whenever they became too steep or too long. The dizziness and the pounding sensation in my chest had frightened me.

David and I agreed that one of our mistakes, besides my failure to hydrate, was that we had delayed stopping for lunch. In part this was a function of the route. Along the Westchester Bike Trail we had not really seen any appropriate places to eat. By the time we headed into Tarrytown it was already past one o'clock and we did not see an easy place to get lunch. My failure to look more carefully for a lunch spot earlier, may have been the result of the fact that I was already feeling the effects of dehydration and not thinking straight. As I picked myself up for the last time at our "resting" point by the cemetery, we resolved to stop as soon as we could for food. David even suggested we backtrack to Tarrytown to find a restaurant. I vetoed that idea. I had worked too hard to get where we were. Coasting downhill heading south would only mean we would have to go back up the same hill heading north. We pushed on, reminding ourselves that we had agreed before the ride to make sure we chose nice places to eat and to take a long break in the middle of the day. The forty minutes lying on the grass in Sleepy Hollow was not the type of break we had in mind. While traveling on a bicycle, even more than when in a car, you are at the mercy of whatever lay along your path in terms of good places to eat. We refused to stop at a Mexican restaurant since neither of us were interested in that option. Interestingly, I do not think there were many Mexican restaurants in upstate New York in 1968; there were plenty of such places in 2018. When I saw the shiny facade of a diner as we entered Ossining, I knew that we had found what we were looking for: a place with air conditioning, plenty of food, and unlimited Coke refills! We chained our bikes on a rail outside the establishment, and took a booth near the window.

David was surprised by this diner and many similar establishments we saw along the way. He did not realize that the Northeast was the true home of this institution. Although there are some older diners in Oklahoma, especially along Route 66, most of these eateries are more recent and are little more than an attempt to copy the "chic" of an American icon captured in one of Edward Hopper's most famous paintings. In the Northeast, diners appear in almost every town and are truly local institutions. The Landmark Diner, where we had lunch that day, was just such a restaurant, serving good American fare like pot roast and turkey dinners. The place was nearly full at two o'clock on this Sunday afternoon. We opted for gigantic hamburgers and fries and struggled to finish our meal. David befriended the waitress, telling her all about how two old guys were bicycling to Montreal. During the early phases of the trip David would expound on our planned journey with everyone we met. After a few days hearing him regale so many people about the ride, I jokingly teased David about bragging. Thereafter, David limited this line of conversation with total strangers. Whether this was because David wanted to guard against pride as a sin or because after watching me struggle for several days he wondered if we would make it, I still remain unsure.

* * *

David's interest in diners convinced me to do a little research after the ride. Historically, diners emerged as a form of restaurant in the second half of the nineteenth century. They began simply enough as a source of cheap meals sold from horse-drawn wagons near factories – an early version of the food truck that has become so popular today. When some municipalities sought to regulate the number of such wagons, wily entrepreneurs made their establishments more permanent by taking off the wheels and attaching the wagons to the ground. After electrified streetcars took over as the major form of urban transportation around the turn of the century, abandoned horse drawn trolleys were converted into "diners," borrowing the name, in an abbreviated form, of the more elegant railway dining car. When gasoline buses appeared on the scene around the middle of the twentieth century, many old streetcars followed their horse drawn predecessors and were converted into diners. During the 1950s diners became purpose-built structures to serve people traveling by automobile. They were an odd combination of the modern and the historic: they often sported shiny metal work to reflect the new rocket age, but retained a hint of the old streetcar look. After 1970 chain restaurants challenged diners across the nation. With menus and structures that differed little from Oshkosh to Okmulgee, such chains had not become so dominant in 1968. Despite the challenge, diners have survived. They are often locally owned and deeply imbedded in the community. We only ate twice in diners on our trip, for lunch and dinner on Day One.

* * *

There are some things I remember from 1968 as clearly as if they happened an hour ago. And there are some things that I cannot conjure in my brain no matter how much I try. Exactly where we ate lunch back then and what we ate remains a mystery to me. When I asked Roger, he could not remember either. I can only assume that we stopped at a number of diners for lunch on that first trip. They were sprinkled all along the Hudson Valley. I have a clear recollection of what we did for dinner, especially for the first three days of the ride. That first evening brought the three of us to Croton State Park. This was our planned goal since our map indicated that the park had a campground. As it turns out, although we were not fully aware of this fact at the time, we had not even traveled fifty miles that day. When we checked in at the campground, the local park ranger, who was in his twenties and slightly overweight, was impressed with our endeavor. He suggested that we have a cook out with him and that he had all the supplies we needed at his apartment nearby. Since this meant he would be providing the meal, we readily agreed. He asked if one of us would accompany him to his apartment. Perhaps unsure of the ranger's motives, Roger and Denis volunteered me since I was the stockiest of the three of us. The trip was harmless enough and I had the benefit of using a regular toilet before we joined my two comrades back at the park. That evening we had franks cooked over an open fire and then sang folk songs as Roger strummed his guitar. Our favorite tune – one we sang so much that it became our unofficial theme song – was Arlo Guthrie's "Alice's Restaurant" that became popular a year later when the movie of that name was released.

David and I had no anthem. After lunch, rejuvenated, if a little over-stuffed, we left the Landmark Diner ready to take on the heat and humidity. David paused to snap a picture of the eatery and I briefly related how Ossining was the home to Sing Sing, a prison every movie goer knows about. I told David that before 1901, the town had been called Sing Sing, but had decided to call itself Ossining to avoid any stigma associated with the correctional institution that gave birth to the phrase "being sent up the river." Somehow, I had known this fact even in 1968 and had often wondered if the good

citizens of this town really thought they were fooling anyone. Ossining and Sing Sing were not that far apart. After
leaving Ossining, I briefly considered a slight deviation of
our route to visit Croton State Park. I decided against alter-
ing our plans. My experience at Sleepy Hollow convinced
me that I had best use every ounce of energy heading north.
About this time I began to follow David's advice and started
to pour ice water over my head at every rest stop. At the diner we had refilled our water bottles, packing them with ice.
With plenty of water and ice, I could spare this indulgence
which was both awfully cold and awfully refreshing.

We biked for two hours after lunch, deciding to call it a
day just as we reached Peekskill. Having left New York around
nine in the morning, Ann and Frances spent the day visiting
the Rockefeller mansion Kykuit and the eighteenth-century
Philipsburg Manor. In fact, they were literally around the
corner from where I was when I had my collapse in Sleepy
Hollow. Now, they were only a few miles behind us and it
would be easier to rendezvous sooner than later. The day had
gotten away from us and it was almost five o'clock. After
meeting at a coffee shop on South Street in Peekskill, our
wives drove us to our hotel in Fishkill, eighteen miles north.
As she drove, Ann explained to David and Frances why so
many localities in the Hudson River region had the word
"kill" in them. "The word comes from the Dutch," she noted,
"meaning body of water, or creek." Once at our hotel, David
and I showered and we all prepared for dinner. We walked
to a diner for our supper that night, although neither David
nor I had a very big meal. We still felt the effects of the late
and over-sized lunch.

When we had arrived at the designated meeting point,
I gave Ann the abridged version of my physical breakdown
in Sleepy Hollow. I did not tell her how long I struggled to
clear my head and I did not mention any pounding in my
chest. Those details could come later. Or when she reads this

book. I did not want to alarm her too much. The day's ride was longer than any of my training rides. It was also further than we biked the first day in 1968. Still I was worried. The next day was going to be hotter. My legs were already a bit wobbly and we had more hills in front of us.

Totals for Day One in 1968
Miles: 47.6
Uphill: 1263 feet
Downhill: 1246 feet

Totals for Day One in 2018
Miles: 61.32
Uphill: 1886 feet
Downhill: 1827 feet

Chapter 9

Day Two

DAY TWO WAS much better than Day One in both 1968 and 2018. There were no additional holes in my underwear and I did not collapse at the side of the road. More than that, the rides in both years were joyous and pleasant. Looking back fifty years, little stands out from the ride that day. In 1968 we climbed our way through the Hudson Highlands along US 9. Regardless of all those hills we never really struggled. Once we got to Fishkill the terrain flattened through Poughkeepsie and beyond. I remember passing Franklin Delano Roosevelt's house and thinking it might be interesting to stop and visit someday. I also recall biking past apple orchards. In 2018, I did not see any apple orchards on the second day, and we did not do as much climbing. In fact, we began the second day by cheating – or as Ann corrected me, making a concession to reality. We had not planned it that way. We had stayed in a Hampton Inn in Fishkill. However, as Ann drove us the 18 miles back to Peekskill, I began to worry about the hills. US 9 twists and turns its way through the Hudson Highlands. During my training I had looked upon the Hudson Highlands as one of the greatest challenges of the journey, remembering all of the climbing on Day Two in 1968. I had poured over Google Maps to determine which would be the best route for us to follow, staying on US 9 to Fishkill, as we did in 1968, or taking 9D and riding closer to the Hudson River. I had even used the maps program to switch to satellite view to see what kind of shoulder there was on each road. I remained undecided until after we drove to Fishkill at the end of Day One. The shoulder all along US 9 was wide with plenty of room for bicycles. That evening the uphill out of Peekskill did not look too daunting. In the morning, I saw things differently and noticed that as we headed south, the last six miles to Peekskill were largely downhill. From the passenger seat I looked at one long future climb. I began to get a sick feeling. Later I checked Google Maps to confirm my judgement. The first third of the trip between Peekskill to Fishkill climbs 633 feet, the remainder has both ups and downs. My problems the day before struck me on the uphills. The idea of beginning the day with a six mile climb and then trying to go 61 more miles, was just too daunting. Discretion got the better part of my valor, and I suggested to David that we skip the planned departure point in Peekskill, and commence the ride toward the top of the Hudson Highlands. He thought that the idea made sense, so at a rotary right before entering Peekskill proper, and at an elevation equal to the Hudson River, we headed back toward Fishkill. When the climbing stopped and we entered into a series of rolling hills, I asked Ann to pull over and let us off. We took the bikes from the rack, donned our helmets, and headed along US 9 for a wonderful twelve miles that sent us speeding down one hill and propelled up the next. In less than an hour we were back at Fishkill, having hit speeds in excess of 34 miles per hour – our fastest of the trip – and without struggling through a single climb. We returned to the hotel to use the toilets in our rooms. Determined to hydrate like mad, I had already finished one bottle of Gatorade from a supply Ann had bought the night before, and picked up its replacement. We each kissed our wives and were soon on our way again.

We stayed on US 9 almost to Poughkeepsie. This section of the road has probably undergone some of the greatest transformations of any that we traveled in 1968 and that we used again in 2018. It was packed with strip malls and shopping centers with scads of chain stores, many of which did not exist fifty years ago. If I remember correctly, this section of highway used to be single lane each way and the countryside was much more rural. Now, it was two lanes in both directions, leaving us with not as much room along the shoulder as we would have liked. It was manageable, however, and the drivers mostly considerate. One or two vehicles passed us a little too closely for our comfort. But there were no near collisions. Also, part of the route has a paved sidewalk that we could use as a bike path – at least according to Google Maps. At the edge of Poughkeepsie, where the road shifts into a limited access highway, we decided to make our way through town on local streets. We immediately ran into a steep hill. After my near out-of body experience the previous day, I became extremely cautious. I stopped and we walked up the hill. We followed Academy Street into the central part of town, gliding past a host of nineteenth-century homes that both of us found amazing. Many had excellent gingerbread work painted to perfection. Once in "downtown" Poughkeepsie we picked our way, GPS in hand, to the north end of town and once again followed US 9.

Here the road took on more of the appearance of what I remembered from 1968: it was single lane each way with generous shoulders for bicycles. This section of the road had stood out in my memory. The Culinary Institute of America was new to the location, having purchased an old Jesuit institution in 1970 and it opened its gastronomical doors in Hyde Park in 1972. But next door is Roosevelt's home, which was already a national historic site in 1968. Fifty years ago I viewed the large building from a distance. In 2018, as an avid national park fan, I knew that the visitor center would have great bathrooms. So I suggested to David that we cross the street and pedal down the long drive to use the facilities.

When David took his turn going inside, I chatted with a groundskeeper. Without David around, I could do a little bragging. I told this young man about our projected journey. He turned to me and asked, "Can I ask you one question?" When my children would ask me this question when they were young, I would teasingly reply "yes, you just did." I was more polite to the groundskeeper who was in his thirties. I said "sure." He queried: "How old are you?" I chuckled and proudly replied, "Sixty-seven!" I continued, "My friend is only sixty." He exclaimed "Wow, I can only hope that I am in your shape when I am that old." With that, David and I shoved off to take some photos at the FDR National Historic Site before returning to US 9. Much relieved, and my ego massaged, we headed north again.

Ann and Frances arrived at Hyde Park about an hour later to sign up for a tour and to see the FDR library. Although they enjoyed this visit, they were a little disappointed that they were not allowed to go upstairs and see the bedrooms. The ranger explained that it was too hot to permit the general public admission to a part of the house which was not air conditioned. When Ann and Frances reported this fact to us at dinner that evening, I was immediately reminded of one of the most profound changes in American living standards in the last half century – air conditioning. Although modern air conditioning was invented in 1902, in the first part of the twentieth century even the homes of the most affluent and elite families, like the Roosevelts, were constructed without any mechanical cooling devices. During the 1920s air conditioning appeared in movie houses to help attract crowds and during the 1930s many offices and department stores became air conditioned. By the late 1940s single family home owners could buy air conditioners, but as late as 1965 only ten percent of all American homes had air conditioning; by 2007 that number had increased to eighty-six percent. Without air conditioning, the great population shift to the Sunbelt would have been impossible. The rust belt might never have rusted, Florida would have remained a swamp, Arizona would still be desert, and no one would have wanted to move to Texas or Oklahoma. The Brooklyn home where I grew up did not have air conditioning, and I do not recall ever feeling desperate for a break in air conditioning on the 1968 ride (admittedly the weather was much cooler that summer). In 2018, David and I often sought brief respites in air conditioned restaurants and stores along the way.

Back on the road after using the air conditioned bathrooms of the Hyde Park visitor center, we began looking for a diner for lunch. We could not find any. When we pulled into Rhinebeck, another fabulously picturesque village in the Hudson Valley, there were several restaurants. The problem was that these bistros were a little too upscale for us. I scanned one menu posted outside and shouted over to David, "Hey they have $16.00 hamburgers here." David, who is careful with his pennies, did not hesitate in his response "Guess we are not eating there!!" We magnified our Google Maps to see if there was a more appropriately priced place to eat located off the main drag. David found a bagel store a half block away and we enjoyed a great lunch. I had a bagel with scrambled eggs and sausage for a fraction of what the fancy restaurants would have charged – assuming, of course, that they would have served two haggard old guys drenched in sweat wearing too-tight spandex without underpants.

While eating my bagel, my phone dinged. It was a text message from my daughter in Alberta, Canada. Before leaving for the trip, she had walked her parents through the process of setting up an app that would enable Ann to track me all day. We also arranged for my two children and a friend back in Norman, to follow my progress. Some people are worried about their privacy and complain that Apple, Google, marketers, the FBI, the CIA, the Russians, the Chinese, almost anyone, can track them through their handheld device. As far as I am concerned, they can all follow me if they want, if the same technology allows Ann and my family to know where I am. And, there is something endearing about my daughter's text. She asked, in a testament to the power of new technology, "Hey Dad, are you enjoying your bagel?" My response was, "Absolutely!"

* * *

This near constant communication did not exist in 1968. On that ride, Denis, Roger, and I were almost entirely on our own. We had no immediate back up. I guess if we became desperate and had a serious problem, we could have found a phone somewhere and called our parents. Fortunately, we never had to. We did "report in" every evening. Long distance phone calls were expensive in the 1960s. Rather than each of us taking turns at a phone booth, one of us would call our own parents collect (that is the person who receives the call pays for it) and provide an update as to where we were and how we were doing. Then that parent would call the other parents and relay the information.

I have often wondered, as a parent myself, how my mother and father really felt about my biking to Montreal. And, I might add, ever since that ride, whenever I have told anyone about being seventeen and biking to Montreal, I am almost inevitably asked, "and your mother let you go?" My mother's answer was that she was tricked. She later recalled that I had elicited from her the promise that if Roger and Denis were allowed to go, then she would let me go too. She thought that someone else's mother would have sense enough to veto the trip. She also claims she found out about the "trick" on the relay phone calls she had with the other mothers. Each had made the same promise to their sons, operating under the assumption that someone else's mother would be the "heavy" and say no. Personally, I do not think that this "trick" explains why our parents gave their permission for the journey. All three of us were younger siblings whose older siblings had already worn our parents down. Even today, parents are more likely to be more careful with an older child. Rules get stretched and broken as more and more children are added to a family. Moreover, we were fairly responsible seventeen-year-olds who had demonstrated our ability to be on our own during the practice rides to Bear Mountain and to northern New Jersey. All three of us also came from blue collar families in an era when working-class children often went unsupervised and were left to their own devices. Allowing us to assert this independence, in other words, was not that surprising given where and when we grew up.

* * *

With Ann and Frances beginning their tour of Hyde Park a few miles behind, and having taken in an injection of protein in the guise of eggs and sausage, and with replenished water supplies, courtesy of the young woman behind the counter of the bagel place, we returned to the road. We did great that day and, even if during the last six or seven miles I walked up hills I might have easily handled in the morning. A few minutes after four, we pulled into Hudson,

New York, with the odometer just clearing 67 miles. We stopped at a park in the middle of town, found a bench in the shade, and waited for our wives who were only about twenty minutes away – again technology allowed us to follow them, while they tracked us. We had texted them earlier to let them know that we expected to get to Hudson by 4:30.

I was a little nervous in Hudson since there were a handful of other denizens out in the heat who looked a little worse for wear either through the use of alcohol or drugs or both. One of these men addressed us as we passed and uttered a few harmless words that unfortunately are likely to be true. This individual, who may have been in his late thirties, took one look at us and said "God Bless you, you are probably going to outlive me." I felt guilty about being nervous when I first spied him. Having grown up in New York City, my standard reaction to people in his condition is to "not engage." So I mumbled a muted response and we moved on to the shady bench fifty feet away. Our wives soon appeared and we began what was becoming our daily ritual at the end of the day: kissing our wives, loading the bikes, drinking more water, and then sitting in the back of the minivan while Ann and Frances drove us to the hotel. As we pulled out of the parking spot and began to drive along the town square, our friend who had predicted his own demise, got up from his bench, took a few steps toward us, then stood straight up at attention, and snapped into a salute. I shall long remember that salute, and my own embarrassment on not responding more positively to this young man.

The most memorable part of Day Two in 1968 also came at the end of the ride. It occurred when we reached our destination at a campground in Staatsburg (the park is now called Mills Norrie State Park). The campsite sat on a bluff overlooking the Hudson. Down below was a marina. We needed to get some dinner and we reasoned that the marina should have a little canteen for us to buy a meal. We were wrong. There was nothing there for us to eat. Moreover, it was beginning to get dark and there was no way we could ride our bikes in search of a restaurant. As we stood by the marina office trying to figure things out, we resolved that we would go to bed hungry. When we were planning the trip, we had assumed that we might have to skip dinner on some evenings. For three ravenous teens we were in good spirits and were even joking about our plight. Just then, an elderly man, overhearing our conversation, approached us and said that he might be able to give us some food on his boat. The man looked ancient – maybe he was sixty-seven. We went with our benefactor, his name was "Mr. Livingston," to his cabin cruiser where he served us scrambled eggs and bacon. Roger and I chatted with the old man as we ate our dinner. Mr. Livingston related how he was retired and was using his leisure time on his boat. He even described how it was possible to sail his cabin cruiser all the way to Canada following rivers, canals and lakes. Denis in the meantime said nothing and scarfed down seconds and even thirds. At the end of the meal we thanked Mr. Livingston and then returned uphill to our campsite. I do not remember singing that night.

I was surprised in 2018 that for the second time, we had beaten the progress of the 1968 ride. In fact, Hudson was much further along than I expected to get on the second day. I should have known better since we were about 135 miles from our start point. This distance put us right on schedule for 67 miles a day. However, we now had to drive 50 miles back to Fishkill and our hotel that night. The drive took over an hour. This meant that the return would chew up the same amount of time in the morning, cutting into cooler biking weather. As we were speeding along the Taconic Parkway, my phone dinged with a message from my daughter. She was tracking us again from Alberta and was worried that something had happened that caused us to be heading south that fast. I sent her a text that explained my error in calculations.

Her response and the drive south, made me worry that my error was going to create a problem for the next day. Not only would we have to retrace our steps to return to a start spot in Hudson, but Ann would be spending half the morning driving back and forth before she could begin her touring with Frances.

Totals for Day Two in 1968
Miles: 58.2
Uphill: 2057 feet
Downhill: 2001 feet

Totals for Day Two in 2018
Miles: 67.32
Uphill: 1,283 feet
Downhill: 1,831 feet.

Chapter 10

Day Three

WHILE WE ENJOYED wonderful rides for all of Day Two in 1968 and 2018, the same cannot be said for Day Three. Even if most of the day the cycling went well, we faced physical challenges and had trouble finding our way – we were never actually lost – on both rides. In 1968, the weather was fine. We had no malfunctions with our bikes. We just cycled forever. The plan was to spend the night in Schenectady with the son of the owner of a delicatessen across the street from where Denis lived. Neither Roger nor I knew the owner or the son. But Denis said the father had arranged the whole thing. The problem was that the guy lived in Schenectady, or so we believed, and that was about fifteen miles east of our planned route. A free place to stay, possibly with beds, convinced us to reach Schenectady before nightfall. Eventually we made it to our destination, but despite our efforts, our ride lasted into the night and, according to our calculations at the time, totaled 110 miles. (When I traced our route on Google Maps, the total was only 98 miles). In 2018 the problem was the weather. It was really hot. As I told David, riding our bikes would be great if it weren't for the three Hs from Hell: Heat, Humidity, and Hills. The heat and humidity, the feels-like temperature reached to 104 this day, made the hills especially difficult. Any time the upward slope became too great, I coasted to a stop and hopped off the bike and walked. I did not want a repeat of the first day when matter came crashing in over my mind.

We began the 1968 ride 33 miles south of the City of Hudson, our start point in 2018. We followed US 9 north, past the sign for the Old Rhinebeck Aerodrome, an airplane museum which opened its doors in 1966 and is still a tourist attraction over fifty years later. The road and the countryside here had not changed significantly in the half century that separated my two rides. In 1968, when we approached Hudson we coasted down to the old river port, and easily climbed the hill on the other side. In 2018 we began the day by cheating, again, but only for a mile. Instead of beginning in downtown Hudson, where we left off the day before, we started at the Fairview Shopping Plaza about a mile out of town. We avoided an initial climb out of Hudson, saving about 150 feet of uphill. We could also avail ourselves of a convenient bathroom in a Burger King. Unfortunately, because of my miscalculations arranging hotels, we wasted over an hour by driving to the start point. As a result, it was almost 9 o'clock before we began the day's journey. During the first few miles of biking in 2018, the sides of the road were crowded with one strip mall after another. The facades of these strip malls told an odd tale of their rise and decline over the past fifty years. There were few of these retail establishments in 1968; by 2018 several had seen better days. Some were even boarded up. Others remained viable, even if they were not that busy on this particular steamy morning.

A few miles north of Hudson, our path in 2018 diverged from the route we followed in 1968. Google Maps, and the road signs, suggested that we follow State Highway 9J, which was designated as New York State Bicycle Route 9. There was no such separate designated bikeway fifty years earlier. In 1968 we remained on US 9 at this point. The 1968 route was hillier, but about the same distance to Albany. Those extra hills were not a problem to my seventeen-year-old body. The sixty-seven-year-old was more careful and grateful that our course had fewer ups and downs. On both trips some of the scenery was truly incredible. As David exclaimed that morning, this was the kind of riding most people dream about. New York State 9J was truly bucolic (as was the US 9 route in 1968), and had the benefit of almost no traffic. Half the vehicles that passed us on 9J were dump trucks going to and from a construction site. These gave us a wide berth, and provided a cooling breeze as they roared on their way. Our first major rest, shortly after my first walk up a hill, was in Stuyvesant near a cemetery. I thought this stop ironic given that the last cemetery at which we "rested" was when I almost passed out in Sleepy Hollow. On this day we chose the graveyard location not because I was desperate and dizzy; rather it was because it offered some shade. It also featured old tombstones, including at least one from 1812. Just down the road was the old church itself, and across the way stood the old rectory which had apparently been bought by someone with money since the nineteenth-century gingerbread sported a recent paint job in browns and yellows. I drank my Gatorade and ate a Cliff Bar. David was busy snapping pictures.

Memory is always tricky and I can recall only a few specific events from Day Three in 1968. I can still see in my mind's eye the vivid image of a gas station we stopped at around noon to get water, use the bathrooms, and, I presume, pick up something to eat. We chatted with some of the locals and this one young man, perhaps a couple years older than us, was dismissive of our ride, claiming he had biked all the way from New York City in one day. It had taken us two and a half days to get to this spot, which was about 125 miles from the city. There was no way we believed him. I did keep his claim in mind as we approached the century mark later that day. One hundred miles in the saddle makes for sore butts and was not to be taken lightly. My recollections from the 2018 version of the trip are more numerous. Not only are they recent, but I also wrote notes on a laptop in the evenings. There were no laptops in 1968. But if they did exist back then, I would not have carried one. Besides, I was seventeen and certainly would not have written anything down anyway. As it was, I had no paper and I probably did not even have a pen on me.

While refreshing ourselves by the graveyard in Stuyvesant, David and I began to wonder, with the heat and humidity building, how we would get through the day. It helped that 9J made its way downhill to the Hudson, and then ran parallel to the river all the way to Albany. There were some hills, but for the most part we could gain enough speed going downhill to carry us through the uphill. As David explained in his best engineering voice, it was all about "creating as much kinetic energy (energy of motion) as possible going downhill that would then convert into potential energy (energy of elevation) by carrying us up a portion, or ideally the majority, of the next hill without much exertion" on our part. That sounded great I thought, as David explained this for the fourth time, but I still prefer to cite Gilje's First Gravitational Law of Bicycling: what goes down, must go up.

David and I made it to Rensselaer by noon, where we stopped at a Rite Aid for a bathroom break. David also bought additional Gatorade. Whereas I packed several bottles with me for the whole day, and thus carried extra weight, David preferred to replenish his supply as he went along. Large chain drug stores like Rite Aid were only beginning to develop in 1968. This particular store was almost new and was big, offering a pharmacy, beauty and hair products, toys, and a whole panoply of merchandise at reasonable prices. The air conditioning was so chilly in this building that I could not remain in the store for more than the few minutes it took me to walk to the bathroom and relieve myself. My shirt, of course, was saturated with sweat which only made me even colder inside the store. We left the Rite Aid, picked our way through the streets to the river and a bridge into Albany with a section set off for bicycles and pedestrians. This bridge did not exist in 1968. Roger, Denis, and I used an older one, sharing it with motorized vehicles, breaking off from US 9 and heading to our fate in Schenectady.

Unlike our experience in 1968, David and I did not have to battle any traffic on a bridge or immediately thereafter. We simply coursed down a ramp to find a wonderful bike path that ran only a few feet from the Hudson. We followed this trail, often shaded by trees and experiencing a slight breeze at our backs, for the next ten miles. Eventually the path ended and left us on the streets of Westervelt. I checked my Google Maps and saw that on 16th Street there was a McDonald's, less than a mile ahead of us. We agreed that it would be an ideal lunch spot. After we got there, my daughter once again chimed in as she traced our path. She texted: "Ooh McDonalds Lunch of champions." To which I responded "And your Dad is a champion." Always wanting to get the last word, she gleefully responded "Yes you are!" Of course my daughter was being facetious and was mocking our choice of restaurant. Although McDonald's is one of the premier fast food chains in the world, and provides consistent inexpensive reasonable quality food and has generally clean toilets, it was not quite the type of restaurant we had hoped to find. Given the day, it was the right place at the right time.

* * *

We did not stop at any McDonald's in 1968. During

the 1960s the chain was just beginning its great conquest of the fast food world. Richard and Maurice McDonald had opened their first fast food restaurant in 1948 in California and profited from the new expansion of America's car culture. In 1955 salesman Ray Kroc convinced the McDonald brothers to let him franchise their restaurant and use their formula for success: self service counters, ready-made hamburgers and inexpensive prices. The entrepreneurial Kroc added to this formula by insisting on a consistent menu across the franchise, a standardized look, and a family atmosphere. Kroc bought the McDonalds brothers out of the company for $2.7 million in 1961. Although McDonald's began in California and continued to have a strong presence there, in the 1960s the company was really centered in the suburban Midwest. The first McDonald's in New York State appeared near Buffalo in 1959. Kroc avoided having restaurants in urban areas and the company did not open a restaurant in New York City until 1972. In 1968, the franchise opened its thousandth location; few if any lay along our route through the Hudson Valley and into northern New York and Canada. Today the chain is ubiquitous with almost 800 franchises in New York, over 14,000 in the United States, and about 35,000 across the globe.

David and I also had divergent experiences with McDonald's. Although I ate hamburgers in high school, I avoided any from a fast food restaurant since I am a meat and bread fan. I dislike the special sauce used by McDonald's and I abhor pickles and cheese. I probably did not eat a McDonald's hamburger until the 1980s when it became possible, in response to Burger King's "Have it your own way" advertising campaign in 1973, to order a hamburger plain. David, on the other hand had worked in a McDonald's from 1974 to 1976 when he was in high school. We talked about that experience as we sat eating our lunch. I asked him what he did as a McDonald's employee. He flipped hamburgers, cooked the fries, took orders, and manned the register. He also had more grunt jobs like cleaning the restrooms, and emptying the garbage cans. As a teenage boy who was running track, he eagerly gobbled up the day's leftovers at closing time. He had been impressed with the company's structure and organization, but he became convinced – fortunately for the world of clean water – that college was the place for him. As for this particular McDonald's, he was surprised at the number of its workers, but noted that most of them were scurrying about filling orders for the drive-thru customers. There was only one person operating the register inside. Although the chain began as a drive-in restaurant, it was not until the mid 1970s, just as David was moving on to bigger things, that McDonald's drive-thrus became standard.

* * *

After sitting in the air conditioning and filling our water bottles full of ice, and our bellies with burgers and fries, we ventured back into the heat around 2:30. Our aim was to get to Bemis Heights, the location of the great Battle of Saratoga during the Revolutionary War. This goal was a mere 54 miles from our start point in Hudson and would be a short day for us. Things went fine for a few miles after lunch, but as we neared where the Mohawk River empties into the Hudson, we got lost. We were following bikeway signs on the street. Unbeknownst to us, these signs were sending us to a trail along the Mohawk. I stopped and checked my Google Maps several times and finally realized we had gone too far west. Somehow we needed to head north and hook up with US 4, which would take us all the way to our day's destination. But we could not find our way across either the Mohawk River or the Erie Canal, despite our combined map reading skills. Perhaps our brains were already getting muddled from the heat and humidity. Every time I stopped to look at my iPhone, I could feel the sun pounding on my head and the sweat oozing out of my body. We knew exactly where we were. We could see what streets we needed to take. And yet somehow we could not find our way. Our personal difficulties were compounded by the fact that when the map indicated we should turn left, we saw a dead end sign on the street. We concluded the map was wrong, or that we were coming at the intersection from the opposite direction, and went right instead of left. After double checking our Google Maps again and again, I decided to let Siri do the talking. She led us back to the corner of Cannon and Veterans Memorial Parkway where we first saw the dead end sign. I said "let's give it a shot because that is what the lady on the computer is telling us." David was skeptical. As we headed down the street, we almost turned back since it really looked like we were on a road to nowhere. We persisted, fortunately. At the end of the block, no motor vehicle could continue. It was a not a thru street – for cars. But there was a park and a walkway that might possibly be a bike path. It led us to a footbridge across the Mohawk and to a bridge over the Erie Canal. I pointed out to David that we were at the very beginning of the canal. As a historian, I viewed the canal, which was completed in 1825, as a mechanism for changing the history of New York State and the nation. This waterway connected the developing Midwest to the East Coast. David saw it as an engineering masterpiece and would have loved to have visited the first lock which we could see from the bridge. Alas, we had already wasted time getting lost and the heat index was steadily climbing. We pushed on, and, after a few twists and turns on the streets of Waterford, and in front of a host of new condominiums overlooking the Hudson, we were suddenly on US 4 heading north. We might have spared ourselves all of the trouble getting to this point had we asked for directions. Shortly after we took our first wrong turn, we saw a group of teenage boys walking on the street. After we made it to the correct bike path and crossed the Mohawk and the Erie Canal, we saw them again. They obviously had known which way to go. If only we had stopped to talk to them earlier. Men, however, even old men, are reluctant to ask directions.

At about mile 49, this calculation includes the three miles or so we biked when we were misdirected, we stopped at a wonderful rest area with a small neo-classical pavilion and a shaded bench overlooking the Hudson. There were also great bathrooms. I thought about calling it quits there. David, however, wanted to continue to Stillwater. A town of that name in Oklahoma is where rival Oklahoma State University is located. David thought ending the day in Stillwater would have symbolic meaning for two University of Oklahoma professors from Norman. I was not interested in that symbolism. We did not make it. The heat index was over 100 and I was getting weaker. We pulled into a Price Chopper supermarket parking lot in Mechanicsville. The name of this town was more meaningful to me as a historian than David's preferred destination.

* * *

Before the American Revolution the word mechanic referred to any laboring man who worked with his hands who was not a farmer. It was considered a demeaning term and a way to identify an individual as having a low status. The democratic impulse that accompanied the Revolution altered how Americans used the word. Since mechanics had played a vital role in the opposition to British imperial measures and in the independence movement, the word began to be used positively. Mechanics came to be viewed as the equal to any would-be aristocrat and vital to a productive society. Even when master craftsmen became entrepreneurs, they clung to their mechanic identity, exemplified most famously in John Singleton Copley's portrait of Paul Revere. As a legacy of this shift in understanding the role of common men during the early republic, eleven states today claim towns with the word mechanic in their name, and three states –

Ohio, Pennsylvania, and Virginia have both a Mechanicsville and a Mechanicsburg.

* * *

Having once written an essay on the subject, and remembering that in my youth my carpet-installer uncle could still refer to a skilled worker in his trade as a "mechanic," I plopped myself down in a town whose name had far greater meaning to me than Stillwater. In the meantime, David called our wives. Because Ann knew approximately where and when to pick us up, she was only a few minutes away. She and Frances had toured the Vanderbilt mansion, but skipped Val-Kill, Eleanor Roosevelt's cottage so that they could make the rendezvous in time.

When Ann saw me she began to worry, believing that I looked totally wiped. I was pretty beat. I had sat in the shade while waiting for her, dumped ice water over my head and briefly visited the air conditioning of the Price Chopper. It was a 25 mile car ride to the hotel in East Greenbush. When we arrived, David and I had little energy left. Our wives kindly, maybe even sympathetically, agreed to skip going to a restaurant. Instead they went shopping, bringing back sandwiches for us from Panera Bread and buying themselves a bottle of wine to share.

* * *

Our day in 1968 lasted longer and was also marked by a period of confusion about where we were. We had managed to get to Schenectady by evening. Denis had an address, and somehow we managed to get there just as night was falling. The house was a huge old Victorian with a big front porch. Its size should have made me suspicious. Would the son of a delicatessen owner live in such a palace? The neighborhood was clearly a high dollar area, although I may not have really thought about that at the time. I remember thinking it was strange that the house was all dark since Denis had insisted

that these people were expecting us. We rang the bell and
knocked on the door. There was no answer. After waiting
a few more minutes we gave up. Now we had a real problem. There were no nearby campgrounds and it had gotten
dark. Having watched too many old movies, we decided to
go to the police station to see if we could sleep there for the
night. The police station was in an old building in downtown
Schenectady. The police sergeant expressed some sympathy
for our plight, but was unable to help us. We really did not
have enough money for a hotel, and I do not think we seriously considered that option. I remember sitting there and
watching a scraggily old man, who might have been home-
less himself, go up to a Coke machine and buy a bottle of
soda. Rather than using the opener provided, which may
have been malfunctioning, he smiled at us and used his teeth
to pry open the top. Some images remain with you forever
and the proud smile of this man after successfully popping
off the bottle top is indelible. That, I vowed, was a trick that
I would never try.

   We were at a loss for what to do. Denis decided to check
the local phone book to see if our supposed host was listed.
Surprise, he was. After a quick phone call we found out that
Denis had the right street address, only the wrong town. Our
guy, we will call him Joe Santini (I cannot remember his real
name), lived about ten miles east of Schenectady, along the
route we had biked only a few hours earlier. As it turned out,
our host, his wife, and indeed his whole family, had been
waiting for us. Joe drove to the police station to meet us and
told us to follow him as he drove his car back to his house.
It was a frantic ride at ten o'clock at night as we pedaled as
fast as our tired legs could carry us to keep in sight of the
car. Fortunately, a few times Joe pulled over to the side of the
road to wait for us to catch up. We eventually made it to his
house. It was a small 1950s era ranch, perhaps 1200 square
feet.

Joe was a great host. He and his wife had three boys, ages 7, 9, and 11. All had stayed up, excited about the idea that Denis and his two friends from Brooklyn would be biking to their house. Although they were clearly not affluent, his wife offered us steak and eggs for dinner, which we ate ravenously. The three boys were put into the parents' bed and we were given their upstairs bedroom. During the dinner, we were regaled with right wing politics. Joe had a job in a factory nearby and, as I now suspect, was soon to be a casualty of the decline of the industrial North. Perhaps because he already sensed the corroding iron of the rust belt, he was an early version of the blue-collar workers who fled the Democratic Party to vote for Richard Nixon, Ronald Reagan, and, hoping to make America great again, Donald Trump. Joe ranted against blacks and bemoaned the street demonstrations at the Chicago Convention, an event which was news to us. He also proclaimed the virtues of George Wallace. This Alabama racist had already served one of his three stints as governor of his home state and ran for president in 1968 as a third party candidate. Wallace even managed to gain the electoral votes of five southern states that year. We said nothing in response to Joe's political opinions. Instead, we busied ourselves with devouring our late dinner before settling into bed in the boys' room around midnight.

Totals for Day Three in 1968
Miles: 98 (we thought it was 110)
Uphill: 1640 feet
Downhill: 1394 feet

Totals for Day Three in 2018
Miles: 53.62
Uphill: 620 feet
Downhill: 682 feet.

Chapter 11

Day Four

THE AFTER EFFECTS of Day Three were felt on Day Four. In 1968, after our extended ride into the night, we started late from Joe's house. We were west of US 9, and decided to follow State Highway 146 across the Mohawk and then head north to State Highway 50, through Ballston and connect back to our basic route – our lodestar – US 9 at Saratoga Springs. A little after noon, we stopped at a country store and bought lunch. We were all struggling and felt we needed a pick-me-up. After our lunch we had ice cream for dessert. For some reason Denis and Roger then decided that drinking a quart of buttermilk would give them additional strength. It didn't. Before we could get going, Denis and Roger headed for a patch of grass on the side of the road where they lay down with stomach cramps. I will never forget the desperate and helpless feeling I had as I stood there, waiting for the two of them to be well enough to continue. To this day I can hear myself urging my riding mates "Come on guys, we need to get to Lake George before nightfall." When I was lying on the side of the road in a patch of grass fifty years later, I was wondering if David was thinking the same thing. David had more patience than I had as a teenager. In both cases, sooner or later we got going and continued the ride.

In 2018 we actually had an early start on Day Four, thanks to Ann. After seeing us depleted at the pickup point in Mechanicsville the day before, she suggested that we get up early the next day to beat the heat. When Ann and Frances went shopping on the evening of Day Three, they bought almond milk and Honey Nut Cheerios, as well as blueberries and bananas, so that we could eat our morning meal before our Hampton Inn began serving its free breakfast at six. This way we could be in the car and driving to the drop off point by 6:15. It took 35 minutes to get to Mechanicsville and after topping off our bike tires with air, and visiting the restroom in the supermarket, we kissed our wives and by 7:15 we were on our way. I was sure that this was going to be a great day. I had already decided to forego the pleasure of tackling Three Mile Mountain on Route 9N. My plan was to ride to Lake George, where we had reservations in another Hampton Inn, and then continue along Lake Shore Drive (Route 9N) to the beginning of Three Mile Mountain. We would cover around sixty miles, which would keep us close to our goal of sixty-seven miles a day. On Day Five, when the weather was supposed to get much cooler, we could start somewhere along the northern end of Lake George and bike another sixty or so miles to Burlington, Vermont, where we could catch a ferry back to New York State across Lake Champlain. In addition, we would ride in the car from the ferry landing at Port Kent to our hotel in Plattsburgh for another 15 miles. So far, we had only skipped a total of eight miles. These adjustments would elide another thirty miles. Okay, I thought, we would not do the entire 400 miles to Montreal, but we should be able to bike over 350 miles, which would still be a great accomplishment.

* * *

We had also sought to make some adjustments on Day Four in 1968. After Denis and Roger stopped rolling around in the grass holding their tummies, we began riding north again. Twelve miles past Saratoga Springs, US 9 crosses Interstate 87, also known as the Adirondack Northway. When we reached this point, we stopped and studied our maps. The three of us had little or no experience with the interstate system. None of us had a driver's license (in New York City you had to be eighteen to get a driver's license) nor had we traveled a great deal outside of the Northeast. As far as we were concerned Interstate 87 was just another road, only bigger. As we stood peering down from the bridge crossing this super highway, and then looking at our maps, we decided it was a shortcut that also happened to have incredibly wide shoulders that appeared ideal for cycling. From that point US 9 headed northeast toward Glens Falls, before turning north again and coming back to the interstate. Our map reading skills told us that the Adirondack Northway would be four miles less to Lake George (Google Maps indicates it is a three mile saving), and we would not have to deal with local traffic, red lights, and finding our way through Glens Falls. Given that it was beginning to get late in the day, it seemed like a win-win situation. When we turned onto the highway, we noticed a sign indicating bicycles and pedestrians were prohibited. We ignored the sign. We reasoned that we would be on and off the highway in no time. For a mile or so, we pedaled happily along with families heading for their vacations tooting their horns and waving at us, or so we thought. Within only a few minutes, however, a state trooper stopped in front of us and asked us what we thought we were doing. Innocently, we explained that we were taking a short cut and were excited to be riding on such a wide shoulder. He told us in absolute terms that riding a bike on an interstate was illegal and that we had to get off at the very next exit. Our shortcut, he informed us, might very well get us killed. Briefly, we considered not heeding this warning, thinking that the odds were against the state trooper checking to see if we obeyed his directive. We decided against flouting the law and exited as soon as we could. Our shortcut added another 4 miles to our ride.

A few hours later we made it to Lake George just as night was falling. At that point, we ran into additional problems. During our planning in Brooklyn, we had simply looked for little green trees on our maps of New York State, knowing from the key that that symbol represented a campground. We never bothered to call in advance to check to see if the campground was open (something our Lake Welsh experience should have taught us) and simply assumed that we would show up and be allowed to pitch our pup tent. This system had operated fine on the two previous nights we camped. However, Lake George was, and still is, a major tourist destination. A quick visit to "downtown" confirms this impression. The place is full of tacky shops, miniature golf venues, and cheap amusements. This was as true in 2018 as it was in 1968. The businesses may have changed over time, but the essential character of the place remains the same. When we arrived at the campground office, the ranger was not exactly friendly. He informed us that it was the week before Labor Day and that he had no more campsites available. He also objected to the fact that we were only seventeen and claimed that he could only rent a spot to eighteen-year-olds. In all seriousness he suggested that we should try another campground 10 or 15 miles down the road. We were already distraught. When he offered that last bit of advice, we became desperate. We repeated what we had already told him, that we were on bikes and that we could not go down the road 10 or 15 miles at night – especially since we had no lights on our bikes. The man finally gave in, and told us he would make an exception to the eighteen-year-old age requirement and allow us to camp in a picnic area that was a part of the park. He did not even charge us. His only stipulation was that we needed to leave before eight the next morning. That was no problem for us. We pedaled over to the picnic area and selected an idyllic grove of pine trees on a knoll overlooking Lake George. It was the most beautiful campsite of the trip.

And we had the place, even the bathrooms, all to ourselves.

* * *

Remembering Day Four from 1968, I was hopeful that things would go more smoothly in 2018. It certainly started out that way. The first thirty miles were some of the most pleasant of the entire trip. The road was great. Shoulders on state highways are often mixed bags. That was one of the reasons the interstate seemed so appealing to us in 1968. Shoulders might become narrow and almost disappear. Even when they are wide enough, they frequently have cracked or disintegrating pavement. Sometimes they are just gravel. When you are on a bicycle, you have to watch out for all kinds of road debris, including glass, cans, and even bicycle parts. On the morning of Day Four in 2018, the shoulder was paved and smooth. Often, it was wide enough for the two of us to ride next to each other. We zipped through Stillwater and on to Bemis Heights, where I regaled David with the so-called importance of the Battle of Saratoga to the Revolutionary War. I tried to explain to him that the standard text book story was wrong. The surrender of Burgoyne's 5,000-man army was not the turning point in the war and was not the reason France became an ally of the United States. Ever the contrarian, I argued that the French were about to enter the conflict anyway and that the British had several opportunities to win the conflict after Saratoga. David pretended he was interested and I was happy I could play the professor again.

Things were going so smoothly that we almost did not stop for a rest at the end of the first hour. We did anyway, on a shady spot along the road – there was plenty of shade that morning. David used, as the small-town Illinois boy in him phrased it, the farmer's toilet (he peed into the bushes on the side of the road). The route paralleled the Hudson and had slight undulations, but nothing that sent us soaring downhill or had us struggling uphill. After Schuylerville, we recrossed the Hudson and continued north on its east bank. Again, the route was perfect. Pleasant countryside, no big hills, plenty of shade, wide shoulder. There was almost no motorized traffic. It was a sheer joy to ride. We saw some small road kill, and two live deer. We did walk up one steep hill in the town of Fort Edward. When we reached the top, we spied a historical marker noting the murder of Jane McCrea during the American Revolution. We had seen many historical markers and our pace even allowed us to read some of them. States sprinkle their highways with such signs, but I often wonder to what avail. While driving a speeding car it is impossible to read them and if you stopped at every sign, you would probably never reach your destination. No doubt, the signs reflect the interest of a local community proclaiming its role in the nation's past. At first I thought New York's historical markers had all been erected decades ago. The one in front of the cemetery in Stuyvesant, where we rested on Day Three, had been there since 1936. The Jane McCrea sign was of more recent vintage and had been erected in 2001.

* * *

Knowing more about Jane McCrea than revealed in the sign's cryptic description, I told David I wanted to have a picture next to it and then gave him a mini lecture on the subject. The sign merely proclaimed that Jane McCrea had been killed nearby on July 27, 1777, and that "her death helped to defeat General Burgoyne at Saratoga." Assuming my history professor mantel, I told David that this brief summary sanitized one of the most effective propaganda coups of the American Revolution. I explained further, in a test of David's vocabulary, "It was also a story that became embedded in American folklore in the nineteenth century through song, poetry, stage, literature, and most salaciously [this word was the vocabulary test – David passed] in a John Vanderlyn painting in 1804." I described the painting as portraying "the young McCrea, with a low cut dress pulled down exposing one of her breasts, about to be killed by two muscular half-naked Indians." I think David liked that description.

I encouraged him to look up the picture on the internet and told him the painting pulsated with sexual tension. I then filled in more background. "The tale was full of irony since McCrea had been engaged to a young man serving with the British during the Revolutionary War and was on her way to join him, when she was intercepted and brutally murdered by some Native Americans scouting for the British." I told David "The Revolutionaries seized upon this tragedy as a great example of British perfidy and to highlight how the British had unleashed savage Indians on even those who rejected the Patriot cause." From this perspective the sign was correct. "The death of Jane McCrea helped rally thousands of American militia, or so the myth goes, to encircle Burgoyne and compel him to surrender that October." Not satisfied with simply describing the event, I insisted on informing David of how historians treated the story. "Scholars have examined and re-examined this brief episode, arguing that McCrea not only helped to turn the tide of the Revolution, but also noting that she became a cultural icon. Indeed," professors love to use the word 'indeed,'"Vanderlyn's painting appears in many a textbook as an example of frontier violence." I did not stop there, although I probably should have. "At least one scholar has added a gender analysis to our understanding of Jane McCrea. From this perspective, her death represented a cautionary tale in an age when women were being given greater choice and independence in selecting a marriage partner. The subtext here was that young women were inferior and could not always be trusted with making personal or political choices: McCrea opted to marry a Tory, rather than siding with her own Patriot family." At this point I wondered if the engineer in David understood what I meant either by "gender analysis" or "subtext." No matter, I was on a professorial roll. I concluded by telling David that "this terse historical marker just did not cut it." I'm not sure how interested David was in all of this detail, but he had been too polite to stop me.

* * *

Having finished my mini lecture, we hopped back on our bikes and cruised along until we reached Hudson Falls, as picturesque an upstate New York town as you could find. There, we linked up to a bike trail that would take us, with some breaks, to Lake George. The first part of the trail was crushed gravel and went along the Feeder Canal. It was surrounded by trees and was simply stunning. Later, when we were closer to Glens Falls the trail cut through a less attractive industrial area. We arrived at Glens Falls an hour before noon, and were only a half mile from Ann and Frances who were visiting the Hyde Collection in the town. We did not rendezvous at this time. We were doing so great that we were eager to push on. Lake George was eleven miles away, and if it took us an hour to get there, we could easily reach the foot of Three Mile Mountain, fifteen or sixteen miles further, before the peak of the heat in the afternoon. Heck, we might be ready to be picked up before two.

The peak heat of the day, at least as far as I was concerned, was reached earlier than I expected. Once we left Glens Falls I began to weaken. After following the bike trail through Glens Falls, we had to ride on a road for a short while. There was little shade and I began to feel the energy drain from my every sweating pore. It did not help that we briefly lost our way. There was a bike sign on the road that indicated we should go right, but like the day before, there was also a sign saying that the road had no outlet – that it was a dead end. We turned and headed uphill. Halfway up, I stopped to check the GPS. I did not want to labor up a hill to find out we had made a wrong turn. Yes, this was the correct way. We pushed on. Having stopped, I had lost my momentum and now had to walk up my second hill of the day. The heat was getting to me and it was still the morning. From that point, it took us an hour and a half to go about ten miles. I had to walk up almost any hill, however slight, we encountered, including a gentle mile long slope on the trail into Lake George. In addition, my stomach began to bubble and get upset. I needed to find a toilet. I was not prepared to "go" in the woods. There were just enough other cyclists on the path to make that kind of a toilet stop too obvious and embarrassing. It was one thing to step into the bushes and pee with my back to the trail. It was another to find a place to squat and have a BM. I am not a very good squatter. We agreed to aim for the Lake George Hampton Inn, reckoning that if we could not get into our rooms, we could at least use the bathroom near the lobby and sit in air conditioning for a while. We thought that after my BM and resting for a few minutes, we could complete the day's ride. When we arrived at the Hampton Inn, which was right off US 9 as you are about to enter the town of Lake George, the rooms were ready. That was it. I had nothing left. We checked in and headed for our rooms. We would do no more biking that day. After taking care of business on the toilet, I showered, even though I had no clothes to change into. Our wives carried our spare clothes in the car. David went to his room and soaked in a bathtub. We then each lay in the bed in our rooms, wrapped in towels and under the blankets with the air conditioning blasting. About an hour later Ann and Frances showed up with our clothes and food. We ate and rested some more. David told me later, he even took a nap.

Watching me stretched out in bed, Ann told me she was getting ever more worried. She reminded me that only a few years before the heart doctor had recommended I not do a marathon since the abnormality in my heart could lead to problems if I got too physically stressed. He had also said that dehydration could lead to that stress. I lay in bed thinking that Ann might be right and that I had best rethink everything. There were just some concessions you had to make to age and time.

Despite my exhaustion, the rest of the day worked out well. One of the benefits of getting older is that you can afford a nice hotel and a decent meal. As David and I rested, our wives headed for an outlet mall. Also, something we could afford. That evening, we drove to Bolton Landing and had a wonderful dinner at a restaurant called Huddle. We even sat outside because, after some rain, it had begun to cool down. The drive was along the route David and I were supposed to take after leaving Lake George, so we got a chance to take in the scenery anyway. I remembered the road well from 1968. There had been some changes. The town of Lake George still looked a little glitzy as a tourist trap. Clearly many a business had come and gone. The Howard Johnson's near our hotel was still there and looked like the standard roadside restaurant of that chain from the 1960s. The lake shore still sported some incredible country homes. Many of these had been there in 1968. Some were new. Likewise, it was almost reassuring to see a number of old-fashioned motor inns and cabin rentals, which in much of the country have become obsolete, still functioning even though they looked as if they were out of the 1950s and 1960s.

That evening I made further emendations to the plan. I was still a little nauseous and my legs hurt. Even with the twenty degree temperature drop, and thirty degree drop in the heat index, I thought I needed more rest. I suggested that we take a leisurely morning. Everyone supported the idea. My plan was to leave mid morning and drive the car north, past Three Mile Mountain, possibly into Vermont. We would then cycle thirty to forty miles to Burlington where we would catch the 5:30 ferry to Port Kent. From there, we would stay in the car and drive to the Plattsburgh Hampton Inn and get ready for the final push into Canada.

That night I lay in bed wondering if the whole trip was just a stupid idea and that we all might have been better off had I never thought it up. Still, we had biked 225 miles. And we might be able to add another 75 miles. I reasoned, maybe over time Montreal had moved closer to Brooklyn by 100 miles. The world was getting smaller after all.

Totals for Day Four in 1968
Miles: 52.3
Uphill: 1,148 feet
Downhill 1,194 feet

Totals for Day Four in 2018
Miles: 43.26
Uphill: 643 feet
Downhill: 279 feet

Chapter 12

Day Five

PERHAPS IT WAS just the weather. In 1968 we never
dealt with any real heat or humidity. Most likely it was my
age compounded by the effects of the weather. Regardless,
Day Five in 1968 saw my seventeen-year-old self strengthened, while Day Five in 2018 saw my sixty-seven-year-old
self weakened. In 1968 on Day Five we cycled what may
have been our longest distance of the ride with the greatest
change in elevation. In 2018 we did not fare as well. There
was no major mishap in 2018 on Day Five. But after an al-
teration in plans, we put in our shortest day with our second
lowest change in elevation. As I studied Google Maps on
the evening of Day Four in 2018, I began to look at the 1968
ride differently. It was 95 miles between Lake George and
our next campground. That distance does not include a seven
mile detour that I had all but forgotten about. I came to a
new realization of what an achievement the 1968 ride was.
Then, we had no backup. We had no contingency plan. There
was no one we could call to pick us up at the end of the day's
ride. The three of us were out on the road alone. When we
ran into trouble, as occurred on Day Four, we just kept pedaling. On Day Five, confronted by nearly one hundred miles to
our next campsite, we just kept on pedaling. Had the weather
turned hot and humid, we would have kept on pedaling. We
had no choice. I did not think about it at the time. But it was
great to be seventeen when everything was possible. At six-

ty-seven I knew better. When confronted by the *im*possible, I made adjustments.

* * *

In 1968 we began this day by biking along the west shore of Lake George, passing one beautiful country house after another. When we were about half way up the Lake we approached the longest hill of the entire journey, appropriately labeled Three Mile Mountain. We pushed up this hill, but at some point its length convinced us to walk our bikes. On the other side of the mountain, the decline was even sharper than the incline on the uphill. We gleefully glided down the 700 feet, hitting the fastest speed we managed the entire trip. Later we agreed we must have reached 50 miles per hour. Thinking back, and knowing now what a speed above thirty feels like today, I suspect we did not approach within ten miles per hour of our guestimate. Regardless, it was a scary experience. I squeezed the handle bars tightly and thought that all I needed to do was hit one bump too hard, or catch a pebble in the wrong place, and I would go tumbling head over heels with serious consequences. Before we reached the bottom of the hill, I decided to start applying the brakes. I didn't try to stop. That would have been almost impossible. I watched as Denis and Roger on the more stable tandem continue unabated to pull further ahead of me. I was fine with that.

On this day in particular, a feeling of personal isolation, which had been building for days, intensified. I even felt a growing sense of jealousy because Roger and Denis were sharing a bike. I was alone and they were together. Before the ride, we had talked about splitting time between my bike and the tandem among the three of us. That never happened. Denis and Roger did shift between the front and back. However, they never volunteered to give up one of their seats to me and I did not press the point. Roger has only recently informed me that by Day Five he was becoming unhappy on the tandem. Every time Roger sat in the front, Denis would not pedal his fair share and would let Roger do most of the work. Finally, when they reached Three Mile Mountain, Roger had enough and eased up on the pedaling himself. I do not know if they exchanged any words. But Roger thinks that Denis got the message and pedaled more enthusiastically thereafter. I was completely oblivious to this tension. Instead, I sat on my bike, resenting the fact that the two of them got to spend the day together. I concluded that riding long distances on a single bike meant you would have to spend time by yourself. So, I let them pull ahead, knowing I could catch up with the tandem after we reached the bottom of the hill. On a straightaway, my lighter bike could easily go faster than the tandem, which was not only a heavier built bike, but carried almost twice the human weight, the pup tent, extra clothes for two, and most of our shared equipment and two blankets.

* * *

Although in 2018 my training had prepared me for the same sort of isolation, with David I never felt that alone. We had spent decades running together and had shared so much. As different as we were in many ways, we understood and respected each other even as we mocked and made fun of one another. David tolerated my warped sense of humor and my sometimes biting wit. I would explain that for a New Yorker an insult was a kind of compliment indicating friendship. He would occasionally repay me in kind. But the nastiness was not equal. I dished out the lion's share of abuse. Deep down, I admired David. To repeat a point I have made already, he is a genuinely good person who despite being intensely competitive and achievement oriented, really wants to help people and make the world better. For David this ambition is no idle academic dream. He has committed himself to providing clean water to some of the most remote places on earth. His goodness emerged repeatedly on the trip. On all but one day, as we shall see, he let me lead. I made the decisions. He acquiesced. When I needed to walk uphill, he did not remain on his bike and wait for me at the top as I might have done. He dismounted and walked with me. Every chance he had, he would ride next to me so we could chat. He patiently listened to my mini-lectures and pretended to be interested. He always encouraged me. He always tolerated my biking shortcomings. When I thought it would be best to skip some miles, he agreed. To this day I am not sure if David could have and would have biked the entire way, including Three Mile Mountain, had he been with someone more capable. David never complained to me about being tired or needing to rest. I know he was hurting, too, but not nearly as much as me. He was the more experienced biker and the seven years, as anyone who has managed to survive from sixty to sixty-seven can tell you, makes a difference. There were signs that David, too, was struggling. In the middle of the afternoon on Day Four this "young guy" seized the opportunity of bathing in a tub to soothe his sore muscles and every evening he treated his aching knee, injured in his fall in Bolivia, with an "Icy Hot" roll on stick. In comparing how we were dealing with the trials of the trip, I often thought of the old hiking joke. One person asks: "How fast do you have to be to out run a bear in the woods?" Answer: "Only a little faster than the person you were hiking with." As far as this ride was concerned, I was the slow one caught by the bear of heat, humidity, and hills. David was the one who was just a little faster than me.

Another reason for my lack of loneliness in 2018 might have been age. Obviously, David and I are much older than the three seventeen-year-olds who were biking to Montreal in the summer of 1968 and as such are more mature and stable in our personalities. I should add that whatever my complaints about loneliness from the 1968 ride, I am truly glad that I shared that great adventure with Roger and Denis. Our bond as friends was only enhanced by the ride, even if over the years we went our separate ways. On both rides I was fortunate that I was with smart, capable people who helped to make the trip a success.

* * *

In 1968, as we continued along 9N to the southern edge of Lake Champlain, I began a discussion with myself. Such self-to-self conversations are typical of my long distance bike rides. Although I had been using a two wheeler since I was seven, and I had already logged hundreds of miles on my AMF bike, I had never taken the plunge to ride without any hands. Sure, I could ride with only one hand on the handle bars. But here I was, seventeen years old, on this extraordinary journey, and I still could not balance myself on the bike without touching the handle bars. It was almost embarrassing. I did not say anything to Denis or Roger about this. They were a little ahead, perhaps, as it turns out, arguing over who was pedaling harder. I was arguing, too – with myself. If ever I was going to take the leap, here on this isolated road in upstate New York was the place to do it. In all probability, neither Roger nor Denis cared if I could ride without using my hands. In fact, no one in the wide world cared – but me. Sure, if I had tried to ride with no hands on the streets of Brooklyn in the sight of others, and I failed, I would be in for more than a fair share of derision. That was the way it was in Brooklyn. There, verbal abuse was a way of life. So with no one watching, now was the time. We were on a straight away. There were no cars. The tandem ahead. "Okay," I said to myself, "just coast and let go." Lo and behold, I didn't fall. More importantly I soon started pedaling. I continued to practice no hands riding for the rest of the trip and for years thereafter.

Over time, however, I lost this "skill." Oh, occasionally on the commute to school I might let go of the handle bars for a second to check something. But I never "rode" without using my hands the way I did when I was a teenager after the

trip to Montreal. When I was young I could pedal along and
even make turns with no hands. After I bought my new bike
I started to think about riding with no hands again. It would
be a great way to give my hands a break and help combat the
numbness I was worried about. Only in mid August did I
decide that I had best master riding with no hands again. On
a lonely stretch of bike path between the Manayunk Canal
and Norristown I let go of the handle bars. Yep, I could still
do it. But not with much confidence. I worked on it for a few
more rides. As it turned out, I never used this re-acquired
skill. I kept at least one hand on the handle bars all the way
to Canada. I had my handle bar extenders which gave my
hands some break. The nature of the ride this time, and the
fact that my balance is not as good as it used to be, convinced
me not to bother trying. As far as I know, David also never
rode for more than a few seconds without clutching onto his
handle bars.

* * *

As Roger reminded me, in 1968 we had planned to catch
a ferry at Port Henry, New York, that would take us across
Lake Champlain to Vermont. We would save some miles
this way, have the joy of not pedaling, and go on a boat ride.
Whatever our maps might have indicated, there was no ferry.
Only an abandoned rickety old wharf. No problem, we simply turned around and headed to the Crown Point Bridge.
This was another "shortcut" that did not work. At least the
road was flat for the additional seven miles.

In both 1968 and 2018 we crossed into Vermont on a
bridge within sight of the old fort at Crown Point. This was
northernmost of a series of outposts that had been built in
the eighteenth century to mark the frontier between the
British and French empires. I knew little of this history in
1968, and much more of it in 2018.

* * *

Crown Point was originally constructed by the French

in the 1730s and called Fort St. Frederic. Today the state historical site at Crown Point has a few preserved ruins from both its French and British iterations (after its capture the British called the fort Crown Point). In the 1750s Fort St. Frederic was replaced as the southern outpost of the French empire in the Lake Champlain Valley by Fort Carillion (the British later called it Fort Ticonderoga). Here there is a massive reconstruction of what was a classic eighteenth-century star fortification. The British launched a failed attack on the fort in 1758, losing over 2,000 men. The following year, however, defeats elsewhere during the French and Indian War compelled the French to abandon Carillion. Fort Ticonderoga was also important in the Revolutionary War. It was captured in 1775 by Ethan Allen and Benedict Arnold (years before his betrayal), who then shipped its cannon to Washington's army besieging Boston. In 1777 the British recaptured the fort during Burgoyne's invasion of New York. Thereafter it fell into disrepair and was restored in the twentieth century as a tourist destination. Further south, at the town of Lake George, Fort William Henry, which has also been reconstructed, was the site of one of the most dramatic incidents of the French and Indian War. In 1757, the French surrounded the stockade and pounded it with artillery dragged from Canada. After a few day's resistance, the British garrison surrendered with the "Honors of War" granted by General Montcalm. "Honors of War" meant that the British garrison, including women and children, was to be allowed to march unmolested to Fort Edward fifteen miles to the south. Montcalm's Indian allies, eager for loot and captives, did not respect that agreement and attacked the column shortly after the British marched out of the fort. James Fenimore Cooper described this epic tragedy in his *The Last of the Mohicans*, and it is vividly depicted in the 1992 movie with the same name starring Daniel Day-Lewis.

* * *

We did not have the time to visit any of these historic sites on either bike ride. Yet I could not help but think of them, and offer David some brief descriptions, as we traveled through what had once been one of the most contested border regions in North America.

In 2018, the new plan for Day Five was to skip Three Mile Mountain, and drive in the car to the Vermont border. This change would delete over fifty miles from our 1968 ride. That was unfortunate, since once past Three Mile Mountain, the road was a series of gentle hills surrounded by forest along Lake George and then, after crossing over to the Lake Champlain Valley, farms and open countryside. I thought I had little choice. The seventeen-year-olds in 1968 intimidated me – there is no way we could match the distance they covered on the fifth day. To be honest, I should add that the days of near record heat had taken their toll on me, as had the miles and hills. No one thing hurt too much. No saddle soreness. No throbbing hands. No aching back. I was just plain tired as my strength was being drained from me. I suggested, and David, always the agreeable one, consented, that we start at the Lake Champlain Visitor Center by the Crown Point Bridge. It would be a quick 39 miles to Burlington. We slept late into the next morning. The cold front which had arrived from the North, brought more rain, and we saw no reason to start the day wet. There was a significant drop in temperature that also brought a shift in the wind from a gentle, if steamy breeze from the south, to a gusty 10 -12 miles per hour from the north. We now added a fourth "H" to our "Hell" list – headwinds. When we got out of the car at Crown Point it was absolutely freezing, the wind chill must have been in the 40s. I even donned a new yellow bicycle rain jacket. We had decided to wear our New York bike jerseys that day, and one foreign tourist was so taken at the sight of these two old guys sporting New York's skyline across their chests, that he asked to take a picture of us. He even posed for a selfie with David.

The Crown Point Bridge was new. The bridge I had crossed in 1968 had been built in the 1920s. This one was completed in 2010 and looked quite modern. The old bridge had been narrow with a metal grating surface which made biking slippery. We had to share the bridge with any cars that came along. That did not bother us, even though the bridge had only about a foot-wide shoulder on the side. The new bridge had a separate bike/walk way and was much higher. David and I began our day's ride here, walking up the New York side to the middle of the bridge where David stopped to snap pictures. As we stood there, David seized the opportunity to play the engineering professor. He explained that newer bridges did not have as much steel as older bridges, because labor in "the old days" was cheap compared to material, so labor-intensive truss bridges were more common. Today the emphasis was to design bridges with limited labor. After sharing this piece of expertise, which he had told me before, we then hopped on our bikes and coasted into Vermont. David, a world traveler who has been to over 40 countries, had never visited the Green Mountain State. He was so excited about entering Vermont that we had to stop for more pictures by the welcome sign.

Briefly we followed the same path in 2018 that we had traveled in 1968. In 1968 after crossing into Vermont, we biked along Route 17 until we reached 22A, which angled northeast until it intersects with US 7 at Vergennes. We then followed this major north-south highway into Burlington. Although traffic at times could get a little heavy on this road, it had a good shoulder and passed through some incredibly beautiful countryside. In 2018 our GPS and the road signs for the Champlain Bikeway kept us on back roads most of the way. The countryside was just as attractive, but the traffic was almost nonexistent. David often was next to me, even when we biked on the main road and not on the shoulder. On both rides, Vermont provided some of the best cycling we experienced. As far as I know, specially marked routes like the Champlain Bikeway did not exist in 1968. They are a wonderful boon to cyclists, although they often include multiple alterations of course with changes of streets and highways, making it difficult to find your way. We had to pay attention to the signs and rely on the GPS which is aware of the bikeway's path. For most of the trip I kept my iPhone in my pack attached to the rack on the rear of the bike. We ended up checking the GPS so often on Day Five that I finally used the rear pouch on my bicycling shirt. Because I had difficulty twisting around to reach that pocket, every time we stopped to check directions, I would pull up next to David and he would reach into the pouch, grab my phone, and hand it to me. We both realized that the whole process probably looked silly, but no one was watching us and at our age, we really did not care what anyone might think. Despite our repeated reference to the GPS, we became a little confused when we entered Vergennes. My GPS said there was a Mobil Station at the corner where we needed to turn. It was no where to be seen. Instead, as we discovered after we had backtracked, Valero had taken over the pumps.

Compounding the difficulty was that Vergennes sat atop a hill overlooking Otter Creek. The climb was so steep that I had to walk. Making things more complicated, the GPS reconfigured its directions once we passed the turn off, leaving us unsure if we should follow the new directions or retrace our steps for a few blocks to see if the GPS would again put us on the Champlain Bikeway. Noticing that the new route was going to be a couple of miles longer than what the GPS had told me a few minutes earlier, we did an about face, then stopped again to check the GPS. It returned to the original directions and the shorter route. A GPS is great. Sometimes, however, it gets things wrong and you have to trick it to do what you would like.

If anything, the road David and I now traveled became even prettier with a mix of old houses and sprawling farms amid gentle rolling hills. The fastest we hit all day was about 24 miles per hour and I did not have to walk up that many of the inclines. The temperature remained cool. On the previous days we were grateful for tall trees that provided shade. Today, they helped to block the wind. David also, for the first and only time on the trip was willing to lead, intentionally breaking wind – as he reminded me – to help move me along. He struggled, though, with finding the right pace, especially as I often slowed to a crawl going uphill. As I watched David ahead of me, I began to think I really should have bought a road bike. I could now see that David was often coasting while I was still pedaling. He was not only a better biker. His Bianchi was also a better bike.

* * *

In 1968 we had planned not only to take a ferry from Port Henry, but also to catch one in Burlington to ride back to New York State where we would camp. Despite the huge distance we had to cover, we easily made the last ferry. As we waited for the ferry, we met some local teens. Roger's memory is stronger than mine here. He says that after riding into Burlington, we were "surrounded by local kids who were fascinated to meet Brooklyn kids." I can only assume that we had told them that we had cycled all the way from New York City, a feat that must have impressed. Roger, on the other hand, was not impressed with these locales. Revealing his big-city bias, he recalled that the Vermonters "looked like genuine hillbillies. Maybe shoeless?" The ferry took us to Port Kent and we headed uphill to a campground a few miles away at Ausable Chasm. No problem getting a campsite here. This campground was the first one we had visited with showers. Despite the cold water, the showers had no heater, we eagerly took the opportunity to get clean. (I am not sure if we showered at Joe's).

* * *

The ferry ride was a highlight of the 1968 trip. I love being on the water, and I relished the opportunity to rest a little while crossing what should really be considered the sixth Great Lake. Although there is a nice bike path today along the Lake Champlain shore north of Burlington that would have taken us close to our destination in Plattsburgh, I was determined to repeat the ferry trip across the lake as a sixty-seven-year-old.

Given our late start in 2018, making the last ferry at 5:30 PM was not going to be easy. Following the same pattern as the day before, the first eighty percent of the ride was a dream. As the day progressed, despite the cool weather, I could feel the drain of the last several days. By mile twenty-four I was again beginning to struggle and started to walk up more and more hills. David – saintly David – would respond to my apologies for walking with, "no you're just being wise." He was being truly generous. For over twenty five years of running with David, I was seldom wise and more often the wise guy. In the meantime, our wives had decided to go to the Shelburne Museum for the day. They both enjoyed it. Frances, despite her Southern bias, exclaimed how much

she liked Vermont and that she wanted to return someday
with David for a holiday. David was shocked by Frances's
newfound love for "Yankee" country. She had grown up ut-
terly Southern and had detested all things Northern.

At mile 29, I asked David to check where Ann and Frances were, thinking that by then they might have headed for
the ferry. It was a little after four and even though we had
only 10 miles to go to Burlington, I was not sure if we could
catch up to them by five thirty. It turned out, our route was
going to take us right in front of the Shelburne Museum
and that Ann and Frances were still there. We were only
two miles away. Because I was hurting, and concerned about
making the ferry, I called Ann and told her to wait for us.
Less than twenty minutes later we pulled up next to them in
the parking lot.

As we approached Burlington and the ferry I noted two
things. One, there looked like there would have been a lot of
uphill in those last seven miles. And, two, there were multiple defunct motor inns that must have dated from the 1950s,
casualties to the Hampton Inns and other chains who upped
the ante of the roadside motel. Ann drove nervously through
Burlington rush hour traffic, worrying that all the spots on
the ferry would be taken before we arrived at the dock. We
arrived in plenty of time. There were only two cars ahead of
us. When we departed forty minutes later, there were a total
of seven cars on the ferry. We never really needed to worry and even managed to leave the ferry line, go to a nearby
market, get some hamburgers to eat, and return, having only
two additional cars waiting in front of us. The ferry ride was
a spectacular seventy minutes, with the Adirondacks in front
of us and Vermont behind. It was as I remembered it, and
more. Although I cannot know this for sure, it may well have
been the same ferry I took in 1968. It sure looked at least
fifty years old.

That night, I suggested to David that we would have to

cheat again the last day. We would bike from our hotel in Plattsburgh, cross the border and at some point thereafter, rendezvous with our wives. I also told David that Ann had announced to me that she really did not want to drive into Montreal traffic herself. Given all that she had done to make the trip possible, I was not going to argue. Neither was David. Okay, I thought, so we won't bike all the way to Montreal. Getting to Canada would be enough. I was perfectly satisfied with our achievement. As much as I was impressed with all those miles I had biked when I was seventeen, I was equally impressed with what I had done at age sixty-seven. Ann and Frances, in the meantime, were drinking another bottle of wine in the hotel breakfast room.

Totals for Day Five in 1968
Miles: 102.4 miles
Uphill: 3,364 feet
Downhill: 3,671feet

Totals for Day Five in 2018
Miles: 31.9
Uphill: 951 feet
Downhill: 827 feet

Chapter 13

Day Six

WITH THE END in sight, Day Six was bittersweet for both rides. In 1968, after a long haul of over one hundred miles on the previous day, we still had the strength to cycle more than eighty miles on that final day. We raced from the shores of Lake Champlain and across a nearly flat St. Lawrence River Valley. Of course we were excited to be in a foreign country, but we also were anxious to be at the end of our journey. We knew we had many miles to cover and, as seventeen-year-olds, we wanted to finish the trip, go home, and begin our senior year in high school. Although we were not fully aware of it at the time, we were eager to get on with our lives. Everything remained ahead of us. In 2018 David and I approached the day more leisurely. Older, and perhaps wiser, we knew that there was no reason to rush. We set a limited goal for ourselves and hoped at best to cycle half the distance of our seventeen-year-old predecessors. Personally, my vision of the future was ambiguous. I still had places to go and things to do. But I was in no hurry.

David and I began Day Six from the parking lot of the Hampton Inn in Plattsburgh, coasting down to US 9, near Lake Champlain. From there we joined the route that Roger, Denis, and I had taken fifty years earlier. As we neared the border, David and I deviated from the earlier ride. When I was seventeen we stayed on US 9 to US 11, which we followed all the way to the border. We had a paper map which did not show many of the smaller highways. In 2018 we had more modern equipment. Our GPS suggested that we veer off US 9 earlier, ride on State Highway 98 to Coopersville, and then follow smaller roads north to an isolated border crossing. More often than not there was plenty of shoulder for us to ride. And the traffic was so light we could stay on the regular road most of the time. There were hardly any hills. We neither sped along at plus 30 miles per hour, nor struggled up any steep slope. Except for the actual border crossing, we did not walk all day.

* * *

On a bike, your relationship with the road and with people on the side of the road is different than when you are driving in a car. While riding in a car, everything along the road just whizzes past in a blur. On a bike you see things up close and personal. Look down and you can pick out every crack in the asphalt and every pebble in the concrete. Rocks, sticks, and debris come into greater focus. As do people along the way. In 1968 and 2018 we met and talked to people on the side of the road every day. Sometimes it was just a short hello. Other times, as we stopped to check directions, take a breather, or go into a store or restaurant, the interaction could be more prolonged. In both years we attracted attention. In 1968 few people rode long distances on bicycles. Three teens cycling from Brooklyn were a novelty. Besides, the tandem and Roger's guitar strung on his back caught people's eye. In 2018, although many more individuals "tour" on bicycles, including those older and younger than us, I think the fact that two old men in their sixties were repeating a ride I made fifty years earlier – as David and I mentioned frequently – drew notice. On the morning of Day Two we met one young man in his twenties who saw our bikes and outfits and began to relate his own experience on a larger organized ride from Boston to Washington. That same morning, an older gentleman, probably even older than us, asked us how far we were riding. A cyclist himself, he almost envied our plans, declaring "there is nothing like riding on the open road." He then advised us to take the bike path from Glens Falls to Lake George. And so it was, day after day. Although in 2018 our age brought us some notice, and my struggles reminded me of the limits of my own ancient body, at times we would both forget that we were in our sixties. On Day Six, we pulled into a parking lot of a local store for a rest. An "elderly" man loading his pickup with his tools asked where we were going and how far we had biked. We told him and exchanged some pleasantries before heading on our way. A few minutes later he passed us on the road and honked his horn and gave us a wave. We waved back. Dave called over to me and said "what a nice old man." "Yeah," I responded, "an old man in his fifties who was younger than us."

* * *

The weather for Day Six in both years was glorious. In 2018 the day began with clouds, but within an hour we had nothing but blue sky above. Temperatures that started in the 60s only climbed to about 80 in the afternoon. And there was almost no wind. I told David that every day in 1968 was this perfect. I am not sure if he believed me. He responded that if we had had the same type of weather on this trip, we would not have had to make any adjustments to our plans. Maybe, I thought.

For the six days in 1968, the three of us had been oblivious to events in the greater world. That summer the French fired off their first atomic bomb, expanding the "family" of nuclear nations, the Russians led the Warsaw Pact into Czechoslovakia to stifle any whiff of democracy, a divisive election loomed in the United States, the Civil Rights movement seemed to be radicalizing after the death of Martin Luther King, Jr., and young people protested an interminable war in Vietnam. We blithely biked on. Joe had briefly focused our attention on current events when he informed us of the disorder that had raged around the Democratic National Convention that week. We later learned that the convention had been marked by clashes in the streets, with protestors hurling curses and baggies full of urine at the police, and the police responding with swinging batons and massive arrests. Aware of national and international attention, demonstrators chanted "the whole world is watching" as the police pushed them through a plate glass window of a hotel. The three of us were not watching and we put the ordeal of Joe's rants behind us. I am not even sure we discussed his comments or the events in Chicago the next day. At the border, however, we were again reminded of the problems confronted by our generation. Canada had been the destination of thousands of young men seeking to avoid being drafted by the American army. Here we were, three young men on bicycles on our own heading into the land of the draft dodger. We were completely surprised when the Canadian customs officials wanted to know if we were entering their country to escape the draft. All we could say was that we had not even thought about the draft. We were only seventeen and just now beginning to enter our last year of high school. We joked that maybe next year we might return to avoid the draft, but for right now, there was no way we planned on staying in Canada. Fortunately, the officials chuckled and let us cross the border.

In 2018, we were more aware of current events and that made us apprehensive as we neared Canada. Illegal immigration had been grabbing headlines even before the presidential election in 2016. Ever since the attack on 9-11, terrorism was on every international traveler's mind. In 1968 we carried copies of our birth certificates to prove we were American. Now, when you travel to Canada, you need a passport. Border security had become a watchword in both countries. I suggested to David that if he wanted any pictures, he should take them from a distance so that it would not seem like we were planning anything illegal. Despite our concerns, the border crossing was uneventful. The Canadian agent looked at our passports, asked us what cities we were from, and whether we were carrying weapons or other forbidden items. Surprised by these questions since we had virtually no baggage, we told him we were bicycling to Montreal as tourists and that we were staying only a few days. We also mentioned that our wives were driving and that we would meet them somewhere along the way. He remained expressionless. When Ann and Frances crossed the border at the same place a half hour later, and, having tracked us on our phones, mentioned that their husbands had crossed at that spot, the agent gave no sign of recognition and denied that he had spoken to us. Perhaps he could not believe that we were married to such beautiful women, at least that is what we told Ann and Frances. Or perhaps he was just sick of Americans at a time when our president was threatening to end NAFTA and launch a trade war against our cousins to the North. More likely he was trained to be uninformative. Regardless, I was disappointed by the response to all four of us. I had hoped to tell the border guard the whole story about how we were repeating a trip I had taken in 1968. I also thought it would be a hoot if he asked us, in an odd twist to the questions about dodging the draft fifty years earlier, if we were seniors escaping Trumpland and hoping to live Trump-free in Canada. Other than asking when we planned to return, there was nothing close to fulfilling this fantasy.

* * *

Once we entered Canada, I realized I had forgotten how flat the ride would be. Not that I am complaining. Looking back to that last day fifty years ago I do not recall much, other than the rush to get to Montreal. The three of us stopped at a restaurant for lunch and were thrilled to hear some French. We were also struck by the egg-like taste of the water. The waitress, using English, explained it was because of the high sulfur content and assured us that it was completely safe to drink. In 2018, we began the day with aiming for somewhere between 30 and 40 miles. The key was to cross the border on our bikes. We were concerned with our tired bodies, and I needed to be the one driving into Montreal. The worst case scenario was to make it to Lacolle immediately on the other side of the border. We went further, easily reaching Napierville. We ended the ride appropriately enough at a Tim Horton's, Canada's most famous fast food chain restaurant.

A few miles after crossing the border, Ann and Frances pulled up behind us and remained there following us for a few hundred meters – Canada is on the metric system. We did not expect to see them at this point of the ride and both David and I began to wonder why this car, which we could make out in our mirrors attached to our glasses, was not passing us. Finally, Ann pulled out, passed us, and drove down the road a little and stopped. Then, of course, we recognized them. On any other day we would have ended the day's ride then and there. But both David and I were enjoying ourselves too much. The countryside on the New York border had been sublime, with apple orchards in Chazy, and farms sporting fields of corn along the way. David, the small-town boy from Illinois, was intrigued with one farm that displayed a vast collection of John Deere tractors. He stopped to take a picture and I reminded him that he had once chided me for buying a John Deere riding mower twenty years earlier, asking me why I had spent so much money on green paint. The scenery actually improved once we got to Canada. The houses, with their sheet-metal roof and stone construction, had slight French touches. They differed just enough from what had been in the United States to remind us that we were indeed in a foreign country. I was so struck by the French appearance of one stone church, right where we met Ann and Frances, that I insisted that David and I pose in front of it. Unplanned was the fact that we had crossed the highway and were standing in front of a road sign pointing "sud" – the opposite direction to which we were heading.

As we neared Napierville, I began to tire. For the first time in six days, well almost the first time, my butt began to get sore. I started to slow down the pace. I confessed to David that in some ways, despite my tiredness and soreness, I did not want the ride to end and that going slower would delay its completion. Deep down inside, I was unsure about what would come next. By 2:15 we had arrived in Napierville. Perhaps, I thought, we might have made the 72 miles to Montreal. Yet I was happy to get to the finish, even though I knew that David wanted to do another five miles to guarantee biking more than 300 miles on the trip. We grabbed a bite to eat and visited the restroom. I took the driver's seat and we headed for Laval, Canada, where there was a Hampton Inn waiting for us.

* * *

Entering Montreal in either 1968 or 2018 was not easy. Fifty years ago, we ignored the traffic rules to cross the St. Lawrence, and used a bridge which was for motorized vehicles to reach the city. We found our way to the central visitor's center and asked for help in finding accommodations. The building was a "log cabin" right in the middle of a square, surrounded by the tall buildings you can see in any larger metropolis. If it were not for this strange oddity of the visitor center, we thought, we could be in anywhere USA. I am not sure what we were expecting. But we were surprised that Montreal seemed a smaller version of New York City. Other than hearing a foreign language, there did not seem to be very much that was French about it. The young woman behind the counter told us that it was Labor Day weekend, and that the city was brimming with Americans. Housing would be difficult to find. After several phone calls, she managed to find us accommodations at the McGill Tourist Rooms. She was very apologetic, telling us that the place would not be very nice. We really didn't care, especially since we were promised a closet under the stairs to keep our bikes. With directions in hand, we made our way to a block full of row houses near McGill University and checked in. As Roger explained in the article he wrote for our high school student newspaper, "At seven dollars a night we were not expecting much. The McGill Tourist Rooms lived up to our expectations. Bertha, our landlady, was an intoxicating woman. In other words, she smelled like a brewery." As clever as these words were for a high school senior, they were a little too harsh. The landlady was friendly and treated us kindly. The place, however, was seedy and crawling with cockroaches. Whenever we entered the room we kept score as to who could squish the most bugs before they scampered out of sight.

* * *

In 2018 we were in a motorized vehicle so we had no problem finding a bridge to cross the St. Lawrence. The problem was that we were surrounded by thousands of other motorized vehicles crawling along. We had to drive through Montreal and to Laval, where I had made our hotel reservations. As we crept along in some of the worst traffic I had experienced for some time, I began to realize that I should have selected a hotel in the city center regardless of cost. The contrast with the McGill Tourist Rooms would have been stark. We might also have had some opportunity to get a better sense of the city to contrast with my 1968 observations.

I became even more convinced of my mistake when we pulled up to the hotel. It was perfectly acceptable. But there would be no restaurant to walk to. We considered going to the supermarket next door to pick up something to eat at the hotel. Instead, Ann discovered that just a mile away was a huge complex of restaurants in a setting that the young woman behind the desk had described as European. She was right. We enjoyed a wonderful dinner and David and I celebrated the end of our journey by drinking a sampler of Quebec beer. Ann and Frances waited to drink until they could open a bottle of wine back at the hotel.

* * *

In 1968 we did not celebrate the evening of our arrival. Instead, we headed for a laundromat to clean our clothes. We met a few characters while there. There was one African-Canadian who called himself "Blue Boy." As he explained: "My clothes are blue, cause my heart is true!" He did not say much beyond that. In a reflection of our own ignorance, we were surprised to see any black people in Montreal. At the time we were unaware of the long history of blacks in Canada, reaching back to the colonial era. Nor had we any idea that black loyalists had fled north with the British at the end of the Revolutionary War, and that escaped slaves during the antebellum period used the Underground Railroad to find freedom in Canada. Most African Canadians in Montreal, however, had more recent origins having emigrated from the Caribbean during the sixties. In 1961 there were only 7,000 blacks in the city; by 1968 there had been an influx from the West Indies and that number reached 50,000. Today, about one in ten in Montreal are African Canadian. Racial tension increased in the city during the 1960s, breaking out into some popular disorder. Of course, in 1968 we had no idea that the same sort of racial problems that beset the United States might exist in Canada.

We were introduced to Blue Boy by a young white woman who claimed to be a runaway from the United States. Denis had decided to take some pictures of this young woman, who was probably a few years older than us. She was not pleased to be the subject of a camera lens. Fearing her identity and location might be revealed, she threatened to hit Denis and have his camera seized by a gendarme. We were surprised by her story. She told us she had crossed the border by cutting through the woods on foot. In our naiveté, we had no idea that Canada might be the destination of runaways who were not draft dodgers. Once Denis put his camera away, she explained all of this, and listened to us relate our own adventure.

Totals for Day Six in 1968
Miles: 83.6
Uphill: 636 feet
Downhill: 869 feet

Totals for Day Six in 2018
Miles: 41.05
Uphill: 348 feet
Downhill: 509 feet

Totals for the Ride in 1968
Miles 442.1
(452.1 if we rode 110 miles on Day Four)
Uphill: 10,108 feet
Downhill: 10,375 feet

Totals for the Ride in 2018
Miles 298.47
(311.17 if we include our practice ride in Philadelphia)
Uphill: 5,731 feet
Downhill 5,955 feet

Part Three

Aftermath

Chapter 14

Montreal and Going Home

AFTER BOTH RIDES I did not see much of Montreal. In 1968 we spent our one day in town going to the Expo. That was a mistake. We were also disappointed by our one contact in town. We had hoped that we would be shown the sights by a friend of a friend – always a tenuous connection to rely upon. One of our Brooklyn classmates encouraged us to contact a Montrealer he had met as a fellow camp counselor that summer. I called this individual after we arrived in Montreal and told him we wanted to go to the Expo. He responded that he would take us there in the morning. Sure enough, the next day at 10:00 AM he pulled up in a convertible, with a very attractive redhead sitting next to him, and told the three of us to hop in the back. The guy reeked of money and was clearly on a different wave length. He then whisked us away to our destination. During the short drive, I could see that our host occasionally said a few things to us, but sitting in the back of a convertible with the top down, we could hardly hear a thing. No matter. He pulled up to the front gate of the Expo and said "here it is, enjoy." Bewildered, we climbed out of the back and off he went, never to be seen again. I can only imagine that as he drove away he explained to the redhead that he was doing three losers from Brooklyn a favor and exclaiming "why would anyone want to visit the Expo in 1968?" We did not realize this at the time, but officially the Expo, which had been a very successful world's fair, had closed the year before. What was left was a would-be tourist attraction known as the "Man and His World." In other words, we visited a rump exhibit that was a mere shadow of its former self. Within a few years the place would deteriorate completely and eventually close down to be repurposed as a venue for the 1976 Olympics. Notre Dame Island, where the Expo had been, remains a rowing center and a city park, as well as the home to a casino. Had David and I biked into Montreal following my planned route, we would have cycled right past it. In 1968, we were unimpressed and later that afternoon made our way back to our lodgings using public transportation.

* * *

My failures in planning in 2018 meant that we never visited the center part of the city. Instead, we spent one night comfortably enough in a Hampton Inn in Laval, a huge suburb (over 400,000 people) just to the north of Montreal. Although I was initially disappointed in staying there, I have to confess it provided an interesting insight to the real world of French Canadians. The neighborhood was booming, with new apartment blocks popping up everywhere. We ate dinner in the Centropolis, a plaza set up in modern European style with a fountain surrounded by a series of restaurants. Given the perfect weather, nearly everyone, including the four of us, sat outside. When we first arrived, we were overwhelmed by the choices of places to eat. Circling the plaza, I noticed that one restaurant – "Le Balthazar" – featured a wide choice of Quebec beer. I insisted that we eat there. I had not had a beer the entire trip. Looking back, this abstemiousness surprises me. At the time, I was too tired at night to even think of beer. I also worried about the impact the alcohol would have on my ability to stay hydrated the following day. At the end of Day Six, with no cycling in front of me, I wanted to sit and enjoy a brew – or two. All around us the patrons spoke French. If we missed the sights of Montreal, at least we would experience the flavor, literally and figuratively, of life among the Quebecois.

* * *

After one day of not really doing any sightseeing in 1968, we planned on hopping on an overnight bus back to New York City. We rode our bikes that evening through the Montreal streets to the trans-city bus station. When we purchased the tickets, using most of the last money we had in our pockets, we encountered an unanticipated problem. We were told that it was up to the bus driver to determine whether he had space in his cargo hold for our bikes. If he did not think he had space, or if he decided that squeezing our bikes into the cargo hold would damage another customer's luggage, we would have to wait and see if there would be space for our bikes on the next bus – in the morning. In other words, we might not get home when we expected, and could well be stuck spending the night in the bus station. There we were, with hardly a dollar between us, close to midnight, standing next to the bus waiting to see how much luggage the bus could take. Once again our anxiety became palpable. This plight attracted the attention of several bus drivers, all waiting to leave on that night's run. The New York driver remained non-committal. The driver of a bus to Quebec jokingly offered to help us and take us to his destination. We declined, saying that he would only bring us further from home. Finally, our bus driver gave us the good news. There was an entire bin that was empty and he could take us and our bikes. With a sigh of relief, we removed the wheels from the bikes so they could fit, and piled onto the bus. We quickly fell fast asleep. I do not remember if we stopped at the border or if the US customs agents ever asked us for any identification. The next thing I knew, we were unloading our bikes at the Port Authority in New York City.

* * *

There was no such drama when we departed Laval. The morning after the end of the ride, we packed the car and headed back to the United States. Our departure was dictated by David's travel plans. Originally, I had hoped to spend a few days in Montreal to see some sights and relax. David was not interested. He wanted to both fly into and out of Philadelphia and he wanted to return to Oklahoma on that Sunday. I tried to talk him into staying until Monday and to depart from Montreal. "Nope," David said, "the international flight would cost too many airline miles as would leaving on Monday." David also argued that by heading home on Sunday, he would have extra time to catch up on his work and get ready to teach on Tuesday. David was a great riding companion, and was extremely compliant on almost every decision I made concerning the trip. But when it came to money, his German Lutheran background thrust to the fore and he could be quite stubborn. I explained to him that getting back to Philadelphia on Saturday for a Sunday flight would be a tall order. The trip was over 450 miles. Google Maps claims you can drive between the two cities in about eight hours. I knew better, especially since the route would take us through the greater metropolitan area of New York. I also assumed that it would be a bear of a drive after having spent six days on a bicycle. With David digging in his heels on the return trip, I suggested that he look to see how many miles flying from Syracuse or Albany would cost. He did so, and to his surprise, he discovered that he could use the same number of American Airline miles flying from Syracuse as it would cost from Philadelphia. When he made these reservations, he even imagined, wrongly I should add, that since Syracuse was so close, we might be able to use Saturday for some biking if we needed to make up lost time due to weather. That was not going to happen, I thought. With David's plans set, on Saturday morning we left Laval, drove through the edge of Montreal proper and headed southwest along the

St. Lawrence River on our way to Syracuse.

David had wanted to cycle at least five more miles when we finished the ride in Napierville on Saturday. This way, he argued, we would be guaranteed a three hundred mile ride. Clearly, I was not the only academic on this trip, and his anal qualities had begun to shine. As we drove to Montreal on Day Six, he studied Google Maps on his iPhone and suggested that once we got to the city, he and I could stop at a bike path along the St. Lawrence River for a quick bike tour. It was a great idea, but the traffic we hit when we drove into Montreal convinced him that there would be not enough time or energy for any riding for me that afternoon. We both considered biking in the morning. That night, I poured over my Google Maps, and saw several trails in Laval that could take us into Montreal proper. We could then claim to have "biked" to Montreal. In the end, David and I agreed to forego those extra miles. David calculated that the twelve miles we cycled in Philadelphia, easily put us over the three hundred mile threshold. I agreed. I did not point out to him that those miles, or even any miles we might have completed in Montreal on Saturday morning, would mean adding a day to the trip and bring our daily average down. I was content to round up to three hundred miles and brag to anyone willing to listen that I had averaged fifty miles a day for six days.

Perhaps the most important reason we skipped any additional riding once we arrived at our hotel in Laval was that we knew we had to placate our wives. Ann and Frances had spent the past six days accommodating their husbands. Yes, they had done some touring on their own. And, yes, they drank bottles of wine without our help. But the only reason they had gone on the trip in the first place, was to assist us in fulfilling our dream. Whenever we needed them, they were there. Every morning they saw us off on our ride. Every evening they came to the rendezvous. They adjusted their plans to our needs and timetable. In addition, both worried about us physically. At night Frances helped David apply his Icy Hot ointment on his sore knee, while Ann eyed me warily as my exhaustion became more and more evident. They were also concerned about us on the road, afraid that some errant driver, or in Frances's imagination, some raving Yankee, might smash into us in a car. Given all that they had done for us, David and I decided that enough was enough and that we would do whatever Ann and Frances wanted.

Ann and Frances decided that we should drive the scenic route to Syracuse. The trip to Syracuse was only 250 miles and should take, again according to Google Maps, about four hours. Who cared if it took most of the day? We began the ride on the northern bank of the St. Lawrence River, returning to the United States near Ogdensburg. This route brought us to a less traveled bridge over the St. Lawrence River. The border crossing was easy here with almost no wait. We also enjoyed a pleasant interaction with the US customs official who looked at our passports and asked us why we had visited Canada. I beamed "Because my friend and I had biked from Brooklyn to Montreal." This official had a sense of humor, and asked wryly, "On purpose?" I chuckled and replied, "Of course!" I then added that I had done the same ride fifty years before. With the same smile on his face, the agent again asked, "On purpose?" "Yes," I exclaimed, "of course!" After this exchange we were sent on our merry way.

Ann and Frances had planned the route well. All four of us enjoyed the views of the Thousand Islands from New York Scenic Highway 12, before we connected to Interstate 81 near Collin's Landing and not too far from the shores of Lake Ontario. We drove south to Syracuse, where, again at the behest of our wives, we stopped at an Amish furniture store. Ann had told Frances that we had bought Amish made furniture from Lancaster for our condo and the two of them decided that they would like to see what this particular retail store had to offer. From there we drove to one of the great tourist highlights of any visit to upstate New York – a Wegman's supermarket. Ann had sung the praises of these stores to Frances and wanted to show her why it is ranked as the number one supermarket in the United States. Frances gushed with excitement at the size, variety, and quality of the place. She enthusiastically snapped photos to send to her friends and family back home. She even persuaded the butcher behind the counter in the kosher section – not a sight you ordinarily see in Oklahoma – to pose for a picture. Before leaving, she bought several Wegman's reusable bags for shopping in Oklahoma, which she proudly proclaimed would make her the envy of the crowd in the Sprouts in Norman.

We had hoped to stay near the airport in Syracuse, but could not find any rooms. As the billboards declared when we entered Syracuse, the New York State Fair was in town. Instead, we made reservations in a Hampton Inn in Utica sixty miles east of the Syracuse airport. Upstate New York is peppered with cities and towns with names borrowed from ancient history. Think here of places like Rome, Troy, Athens, Sparta, Corinth, Ithaca, Attica, Smyrna, Pompey, Fabius, and Cincinattus, as well as Utica and Syracuse. These communities date back to the 1790s and early 1800s when Americans, heavily influenced by the study of antiquities, believed that United States would be a new Athens or a new Rome and every frontier settlement would become a great metropolis. Those ambitions never quite panned out and many of these places are now small towns or rust belt cities.

The drive between Syracuse and Utica turned out to be a blessing in disguise. One of the reasons David had liked the idea of flying out of Syracuse, other than the fact that he could save airline miles that a Montreal flight would have cost, was that Frances, a tried-and-true Southerner, had one grandparent who had been born near Syracuse. In the evenings, Ann and Frances did some genealogical digging and discovered that Frances's grandmother had really grown up east of Syracuse in and around the town of Vernon. Instead of taking the New York State Thruway to Utica, we followed State Highway 5 to bring Frances right through the heart of this region. Frances, who admitted that upstate New York and Vermont were more beautiful than she ever imagined, fell especially in love with this area of the Mohawk Valley. As for me, I enjoyed watching her surprised enthusiasm as we looked for buildings that might have been around in 1900 when her grandmother was growing up. There were not many. Still, Frances adored the region, texting her sister back in Norman that she would, using a wonderfully evocative phrase that dripped with her Southern drawl, fill her in "on all of the mayonnaise and mustard" upon her return.

That night we went to Denny's to eat and David, ever the big spender, sprang for a dinner for four that ran about fifty dollars. I should not complain. I like Denny's and it is one of my favorite restaurants. I have relatively vanilla tastes in food and Denny's allows me to order a real meat and potatoes meal, as well as a big breakfast at any time of the day. My friend Rob used to chide my penchant for eating at Denny's, especially when we took our families for ski vacations in Taos. Rob would treat his family to some hot Mexican restaurant, and I would drag my family to Denny's. For decades, Rob never passed up an opportunity of making fun of my food preferences, including his not-so-laudatory comments at my retirement party. The next morning, we dropped David and Frances off at the Syracuse airport and then headed south. We stopped for one night at my brother's house near Binghamton before returning to Philadelphia, exhausted and elated that the trip was over.

* * *

In 1968 Roger, Denis, and I ended our journey a day earlier. We unloaded our bikes at the Port Authority Bus Terminal at 42nd Street and put our wheels back on the bike frames.

This task was not easy since the nut and bolt on the wheels needed to be fastened with a wrench. In my haste I did not get my rear wheel on straight, leaving it rubbing against my newly acquired fender. I did not notice this problem as we headed down Broadway. When we arrived at the Brooklyn Bridge, we were too tired to bother carrying our bikes down into the subway station and back up to the bridge walkway. It was early Sunday morning and there was not much traffic. We ignored the rules again and biked on the roadway. This decision created its own problems because the metal grating on the surface left us more unstable than we would have liked. We also created a log jam for what little traffic there was. To accommodate the honking horns, we pedaled even harder. It was at this point that I noticed that I was struggling, especially on the downhill portion of the bridge. Instead of coasting, I was still pedaling like crazy to stay close to Denis and Roger. When we finally made it to the street on the other side of the bridge, I took a more careful look at my back tire and realized that it had been rubbing against the fender, working like a brake. Out came the wrenches. We made one last adjustment, before heading up to Fourth Avenue and the final sprint back to our homes in Bay Ridge, six miles away.

Chapter 15

Economy

ONE OF MY favorite sections of Henry David Thoreau's
Walden is his chapter "Economy" in which he counts up the
cost of his experience in rejecting the material world. These
calculations are both hilarious and ironic. Here is this man
who is proclaiming the virtues of a simple life and attacking
capitalist values, noting every penny he spent. Don't get me
wrong. I admire Thoreau. For decades, each time I taught
the American History Survey I brought a tattered paperback copy of *Walden* to class to highlight transcendentalism
and antebellum reform. I regaled the class with how popular
Walden was in the age of hippies and communes during the
1960s, and how when I was in college I carried this same
copy of the book in my back pocket to impress girls. I read
to them passages from the chapter called "Solitude" in which
Thoreau, with prose that bordered on poetry, described how
he communed with God and Nature. I embraced Thoreau's
attack on possessions in part as a subtle critique of the ma-
terialism of the current crop of students. Inevitably, a few
students in the class would later claim that this lecture inspired them to read *Walden*. Despite this admiration, I think
Thoreau's attitude about money hypocritical. As an old man,
I am also more willing to embrace the possessions dismissed
by Thoreau and decry his assertion that the "spending of
the best part of one's life earning money in order to enjoy a
questionable liberty during the least valuable part of it" was

a waste of time. With Thoreau's discussion of "economy" in mind, then, I offer my own reckoning of expenses in 1968 and 2018. I do so not to highlight the benefits of youth touted by Thoreau – my ride reminded me that those benefits are many and unequaled – but to trumpet the benefits of my old age, having earned enough money to enjoy the *unquestionable liberty* of a *valuable* part of *my life*.

The cost of the ride in 1968 was minimal and much of it did not come out of my pocket. Thoreau, who after all was released from jail when someone else paid his taxes, would have been proud. My father bought my bike for me for $43. I used his backpack which he had from the army in the 1940s. Cost in money: zero. I wore my regular clothes, a pair of shorts, sneakers, some socks, and underwear (with holes added at no extra cost), perhaps two shirts, maybe a poncho (never used), and some sort of pull over sweater for the cool of the evenings. Total estimate for clothing is $75. None of these expenditures was really from my own money. Roger and I both agreed that we brought with us $100 each in cash. I will count this money as my own, although it was probably saved up from my allowance. We used all of our cash for food, camping fees, and seven dollars for our room the one night in Montreal. We spent close to our last penny on the bus ticket back to New York. Total cost, then, was $218 (of which only $100 was spent at the time). As a historian I am not a fan of inflation indexes since prices rise unevenly. The average price of a house from 1968 to 2018 has grown tenfold, while milk prices have only tripled. From this perspective, an inflation index often obscures as much as it reveals. Be that as it may, it is possible to go online and calculate how much inflation has altered the supposed worth of a dollar. Using an inflation calculator, one dollar in 1968 is worth $7.27 in 2018. So an inflation adjusted cost for the ride is $1584.86 or $727, depending on how you look at it. In either case, the price was higher than I would have thought.

The larger number included everything I wore or ate, as well as the price for my bike which I used for multiple years. In fact, the next summer I rode the bike on my job delivering Western Union telegrams when I was not only paid the minimum wage of $1.65 an hour (today the minimum age is only $7.25, less than in 1968 when adjusted for inflation), but awarded three cents an hour for the use of my bike. At 40 hours a week for ten weeks that means I earned a whopping $12 from that bike alone, reducing its cost to $31. Putting the bike and clothes aside, we can focus only on the money I spent on the trip. Cash spent was $100, or $727 in 2018 terms.

The story is entirely different for 2018. For the jubilee bike trip, I tried to spend money with abandon. That was intentional. Having used the best part of my life earning money, I now have the liberty to spend it.

Thanks to another great change over the last fifty years, I can keep track of my expenditures by looking at my credit card statements. Credit cards are handy little devices, which will probably soon be supplanted by our iPhones or even chips imbedded into our skin, but were not that prominent in 1968. What we recognize as the modern credit card is a relatively new development. Charge cards appeared in the 1940s and 1950s, but the first plastic and national card was issued by 1959, and Master Card (originally known as Interbank/Master Charge) emerged from a group of California banks in 1966. When I was growing up, only the more affluent used credit cards. My father did not get his first credit card until the 1980s after he retired and wanted to rent a car when he traveled. His choice was to leave a huge cash deposit, or to charge the rental. As careful as he was with his money, and as much as he liked to see the cash in his wallet, he quickly saw the advantage of plastic. Needless to say, in 1968 I did not carry a credit card in my pocket. Nor did Roger or Denis. We carried cash. If we had lost our money, or somehow spent it all, we would have had to phone our parents and they might have been able to wire us some money using Western Union. This approach seems almost primitive now. On my 2018 ride, my wallet brimmed with several credit cards. I even ordered a new credit card for the trip – a Hilton Honors Card that issued extra points every time I stayed at a Hilton Hotel (like the Hampton Inns). Credit cards issue such points, or pay money back, to encourage their use. The Hilton Honors points can pay for future stays at a Hilton hotel. I earned enough points on this trip to spend several free nights. Some people rely on the credit offered by their cards, and make the minimum payment at the end of the month. These spendthrifts pay outrageous interest and often end up bankrupt. Ann and I have had credit cards since the 1970s and always pay the balance when it is due. This way we can carry minimum cash and buy almost anything we want. Of course, on the bike trip we carried some cash, withdrawn from an ATM machine, another recent financial mechanism that provides access to your bank account almost anywhere.

Using my credit card statements, I know exactly how much money I spent for hotels the week of the trip: $1298.70. We stayed the first night in a Best Western in Brooklyn because that was the only acceptable hotel in my old neighborhood. The Gregory is a nice place to stay, but for the rest of the trip I opted for Hampton Inns. This chain is not upscale, but is decidedly better than most other hotels you can find on the highway while traveling cross country. It generally charges a little more than many of its competitors. That was fine with me since I knew at a Hampton Inn I was guaranteed a good bed, clean room, and a nice breakfast. The service is also usually exceptional and if for some reason you are truly unsatisfied, Hampton Inns won't charge you. I know this for a fact. A few years back Ann and I had an unfortunate sleepless night at one Hampton Inn – a strong wind made the metal facing on the roof vibrate, convincing us, even though we do not believe in ghosts, that the room was haunted. In the morning when we were asked how we slept and said that we had been woken up by this strange noise (we had also called the desk in the middle of the night), the clerk said that the room was on them. In other words, Hampton Inns was exactly the kind of hotel someone in my income bracket could enjoy.

Then there was the food. My credit card lists $250.43 for meals in restaurants. This tally tells only a part of the story, since Ann bought some of the food and I paid for lunch a few times with cash. Although we had our free breakfast at the Hampton Inn – except on the third morning when we left early to drive to our start point – we generally bought a nice lunch and ate dinner at a decent restaurant. Since I had to pay for myself and Ann, the total food bill, including snacks and Gatorade, was approximately $500. This does not include the lunches Ann bought during the day with Frances, nor does it include the wine they drank in the evening.

In calculating costs, we must also look at all of the equipment I purchased. Since I had a perfectly serviceable Trek Verve for casual riding, we should count the price of the Trek FXS-5 that I bought to use on the trip. The bike alone ran $1649 with tax. Additional expenses included two new sets of tires, a bike rack, water bottle racks, water bottles, lights, and a lock. All told, the bike actually cost $2,004.08. I also purchased two new sets of riding gloves, three pairs of riding pants, and three extra riding shirts. We must add in the calculation of the bottom line the price of butt creme. All of these purchases came to $746.24. Total for the equipment was $2750.32.

There were some additional costs. I won't count the wear and tear on my car, but I spent at least $50 in tolls and $154.30 in gasoline (David paid for one tank of gas on the last day of the trip that is not included in this total). In addition, I popped for $106 of David's bicycle shipping charge.

Total miscellaneous additional costs: $304.30

Add all of the costs together, the final bill for the trip is $6151.52. That sounds like a lot of money. Yet it is only $853.88 in 1968 dollars – or less than four times the $218 cost (cash spent plus equipment) of the 1968 ride. Even when I thought I was being extravagant, I was not really a spendthrift. Take that Henry David Thoreau!

Chapter 16

Second Guessing

IN THE DAYS and weeks that followed the ride, I had family obligations that prevented me from continuing to bike. Throughout September I was busy with packing my mother-in-law's possessions and moving her into an independent living facility, while at the end of the month I was preoccupied with waiting for my third grandchild to arrive. Too busy with these cycles of life, there was no bi-cycling for me. In the meantime, David sent me constant reminders of the miles he was adding to his annual tally. The first weekend he was back in Oklahoma he logged fifty extra miles and then on the following weekend he let me know he had managed to finish a century ride. Was David simply sharing his joy at accomplishing these achievements, or was he subtly reminding me of what he could have done had I not held him back? Regardless. All I could do was replay our ride in my head over and over again. As I thought about that trip, for every day I could conjure up images of true joy, where the ride was glorious. And, for every day, except the last, I could recall moments of trial. Although I remained convinced that the ride was a great success even if we pedaled only 300 instead of 400 miles, I could not help but second guess myself. All my life I had been achievement oriented, so falling shy of perfection left a gnawing in my soul that all the rational thought in the world could not fully purge.

I reckoned that I could have trained harder and longer.

Had I been riding distances for a year, no, had I been riding distances for years like David, I might have been able to handle this mammoth journey with greater ease. Since the realities of life, like finishing my teaching career, taking care of my mother-in-law who had broken her foot that winter, getting ready to sell a house and the move from Oklahoma, had prevented me from training earlier, I could have still trained harder. I should have lengthened my rides sooner. I needed to have some long rides of 70, 80, even 100 miles. I needed to do more hills, more heat, more everything. I should have rented a bike when I was in Oregon to ride for hours and hours. I should have gone to the gym every evening on that trip and pedal away on a stationary bike. I should never have gotten sick two weeks before the trip.

In the end, my rational being won out. I trained plenty. I would not give up a moment of being with my grandchildren and being exposed to the germs they always seem to be carrying. Twelve hundred miles got my body ready. Nothing gave in. My hands survived. My back survived. My legs got tired. But six days on a bicycle was bound to do that regardless of what I did to prepare.

Perhaps I could have carried less weight on my bike. David studiously avoided carrying anything extra. He had learned from experience that every ounce counted. He took with him only two bottles of water – one mixed with Gatorade – that he replenished on the road. He had a small repair kit attached to the seat of his saddle. His Cliff Bars and phone were stashed in the back pockets of his biking shirt. That was it. I carried a pannier pack on the rack installed over the rear tire. In that pack I had a first aid kit, a spare inner tube, handiwipes, snacks, and a chain to lock our bikes when we stopped for lunch. I thought this baggage was necessary. In addition, I had two large water bottles and, after the first day, I loaded four bottles of Gatorade in the pack. All told the pack probably added ten pounds. David could have carried some of these extras, but I did not ask him and he did not volunteer. David's bike was only a little lighter than mine. I weigh five pounds more than David, and with the added gear, maybe I was carrying fifteen pounds more than David. I am also about three inches taller than David and that difference should have neutralized the impact of the weight. I could have minimized the differential even further by going on a diet when I was training. But I needed to take in additional calories since I was burning up more than the normal level of energy. Besides, you would think with 1200 miles under my belt in three months, that my belt might have tightened on its own. To the contrary, all that training merely increased my appetite and provided an excuse for me to eat to my heart's content. I neither gained nor lost weight. When I began my senior year in high school I weighed 173 pounds and I was 181 pounds when I graduated. In 2018, I began the ride at 193 pounds, perhaps two pounds below my normal weight of 195 pounds. Although I may have added twenty pounds to my own weight in fifty years, and I am technically overweight, my 1968 bike was much heavier than my new Trek FXS-5 and I probably carried at least another fifteen pounds between my pack, canteen, and blanket. Overall, then, even if you add the extras of my 2018 baggage, the difference was not that great. In the final analysis, I do not think that weight was the root of my problem.

Well, I thought, I could have planned better. Perhaps I should have done the ride earlier in the summer before David began teaching. I knew before the ride, that fifty miles a day was doable. Forty would have been a piece of cake. I should have made the concession to reality earlier. Then I thought that eight or ten days on a bike might also have taken its toll. Besides, I needed the time before the ride to train. And David had scheduled his trips to Bolivia and Germany long before he committed to the ride. Short of riding in July, when I was not physically ready, riding earlier would not have worked. Keeping the timing of the ride was also one way of retaining the symmetry with 1968.

There were other things in the planning stages which might have helped. I had selected the stops each night based on getting close to where we camped in 1968. That was a mistake. I should have calculated the number of miles we rode each day in 1968 and realized that if I simply paralleled that course, the last two days would be monster rides beyond the capability of my sixty-seven-year-old body. In 2018, we did great the first two days of riding, beating our progress in 1968 significantly. Even after the third day, when we stopped at 54 miles in Mechanicsville, we were a good ten miles closer to Montreal than when we rode in 1968. Also, the long trek by car from Fishkill to Hudson on the third day, meant a start close to nine in the morning. Shoving off on our bikes two hours earlier would have given us some more time in the coolest part of the day. We might have easily covered an additional 13 miles that day for the requisite 67. Throw in the additional time in the heat when we lost our way trying to cross the Mohawk River and we could have stopped earlier and spared our bodies the strain of biking in a heat index of over 100. Had I studied the maps more before that day we could have avoided losing a half an hour and riding a mile or so in the wrong direction. Without the drain of that day, the next one would have brought us at least to Three Mile Mountain. Instead, we only managed to get to Lake George. This left us with too much distance to ride on the fifth and sixth days. With that many miles to cover, we had to make an adjustment and allow the car to carry us to a convenient start point, skipping some miles and Three Mile Mountain.

While some planning adjustments might have helped, and I would certainly change things if I did the ride again next year (which neither Ann nor Frances would allow), ultimately the combination of my body and the weather prevented my biking the entire 400 miles. I made hydration ad-

justments after the first day that would have kept me going
had conditions not worsened on the third and fourth days.
Of the three hellish "Hs"– hills – were the greatest culprit
on that first day. My not drinking enough, combined with
some heat and humidity, struck a mighty blow. After getting
dizzy in Sleepy Hollow, I became a little ride-shy. I worked
my way through these concerns and we did manage 67 miles
on Day Two. The second and third "Hs" were devastating
on the third and fourth days. Even though we had the early
start on the fourth day, I ran into the proverbial "runners"
wall: that point in a marathon when the mind and body cry
out "STOP!" Up until that point I was doing great and enjoying myself. Shortly after we left Glens Falls my ability
to deal with the heat, humidity, and the hills deteriorated.
When we got to Lake George, I had nothing left. I needed
to rest. I needed to get into air conditioning. And I needed
a bathroom. Without that drain, I could have handled the
head winds better on the fifth day. The sixth day, with the
temperature perfect, I felt almost like I could bike forever.

Perhaps I could have run through the wall. The standard
advice for dealing with the "runners" wall is to hydrate, to
eat energy bars during the race, to run within yourself from
the beginning, and to be in as good a shape as possible. By
Day Four I believed I had followed at least three of these
four pieces of advice. I was hydrating and eating "Cliff Bars."
And at no time during the previous three days had I been a
"galloping pony" and pushed the pace. Our pace throughout
the ride, except briefly on Day Two when we were in the hills
and gliding a great deal, was never more than my normal
training rides. A less standard piece of advice, one advocat-
ed by some of my running buddies over the years (but not
David), was just simply to gut it out. This argument holds
that beating "the wall" was a matter of mind over matter and
that it was important to push the envelope. I followed this
philosophy in a race when I was in my thirties and discov-

ered that matter can crash in over mind and that if you push to the end of the envelope, you could fall off. The race was on a hot and humid April day in Oklahoma City and I was inadequately hydrated. I kept pushing myself, hoping for a personal best. I began hallucinating, and I suddenly felt myself floating one hundred feet in the air looking down at the race. An out of body experience is not a good thing. I do not remember finishing the race. I do remember waking up with an IV in my arm and the first aide station worker assuring me "Don't worry, you finished the race," and in recognition of the anal personality of someone who pushes themselves too hard, "and we are getting your time."

What did not work when I was in my thirties, was certainly not going to work in my sixties. I knew that from my dizziness the first day. I also thought about a more recent experience with heat and hydration. I had run in Oklahoma summers for over thirty-five years. Most of the time the temperature at noon was near ninety. At least once I ran past a temperature sign that had 100 emblazoned on it. I proudly turned to my running partner at the time, and said "we finally did it, we broke the century," adding, "but that is the last time I want to see three digits while we run." I was therefore shocked when I experienced a bout of heat stroke from a hike in the Wichita Mountains in southwest Oklahoma a few years ago. I was leading a group of college and university teachers from an NEH seminar on a hike up Elk Mountain. This was a climb I had done dozens of times. It was a mile up and a mile down. It was a hot June day where the temperature was going to hit one hundred in the afternoon. I drank Gatorade, but not enough. I should have known I was in trouble when I lost the trail in a rock field for a few minutes on the way down. What really did me in, though, was waiting in line at the Meers Café. This popular hamburger spot almost always has a line out the door – in the middle of nowhere. Our graduate assistant had parked one of the vans in some gravel and we could not get the van back on the road. My co-director and I spent an additional hour in the afternoon heat trying to free the van and then waiting for a tow truck. When I returned to the line to get into the restaurant, I began to get dizzy and had to sit down. I recovered, but my head remained foggy the rest of the day. I remembered this experience at Sleepy Hollow. I also remembered my heart. There is little question that the "runners" wall is all about how the mind plays tricks on the body. Yet, sometimes, there is no trick. At age sixty-seven, I was not going to take that chance. I had been there before, and the results were not pretty. There would be no wall smashing for me.

Okay, so I could have been tougher and I could have planned better and that might have helped us to get some more miles in given the conditions we faced. Ultimately, however, it was those conditions that did me in and prevented me – I won't presume to speak for David – from getting closer to the full 400 miles. I told David that I remembered every day in 1968 being just like it was on that last day of our trip. I wondered if after fifty years I was misremembering things or if everything was just easier for a seventeen-year-old. No doubt things were easier for me in a body that was fifty years younger and twenty pounds lighter, but the weather mattered. I checked the Weather Underground website which allows you to click on weather history and get a temperature reading for several points along our path. During the week before Labor Day in 1968, every day was like that last day in 2018 – only better. Even in New York City, the morning temperatures began in the high 60s. Not a single day of our ride did the temperature reach above 80. I always knew that we were lucky with the weather in 1968 since it did not rain at all the entire trip. I did not realize until now, how lucky we were with the temperature.

It was more than luck. Sure, it was unusual to have a week without rain in 1968. In 2018 we avoided riding in the rain on the fourth and fifth days by stopping early the one day, and starting late the next. We simply watched the rain fall from the dry safety of our hotel windows. Rain aside, the big difference in weather for the two rides was the climate change that has occurred in the last fifty years. Globally temperatures have increased about a degree over that time span. Each year there are great fluctuations within this larger framework. It so happens that those fluctuations were acute when comparing 1968 to 2018. Within the lower 48 states there was about a five degree difference in temperature between those two years. We can trace the temperature shift within New York City as well. In 1968, the absolute high for August recorded at the Central Park weather station was 91 degrees. The average high was 83 degrees and the average dew point was a comfortable 59. Were there some sweltering days that August? Of course. But nothing like August 2018 where the high temperature hit 94 degrees and the average high was 87 degrees. More importantly, the average dew point for the city that month was a miserable 68. The dew point has a minimal effect on the heat index when the temperatures are in the 70s and low 80s. Once you get into the high 80s and the 90s, the heat index begins to zoom toward the century mark and beyond.

I know that any given weather event can not be attributed to the larger trends of climate change. Fred, one of my other running buddies before his knees gave out, was not only the Director of the University of Oklahoma School of Meteorology for sixteen years, but also served as president of the American Meteorological Society. Over three decades of running, Fred drilled into my brain the importance of climate change and how we should never blame the daily or weekly weather on the larger overall trends. As Fred repeatedly told me, the weather is packed with epiphenomena and that what truly counts in understanding what is happening to our planet are the larger developments. Yet I cannot help but think that in this case, my dizziness on the first day, my struggles in the heat thereafter, and my riding into the "wall" on the fourth day, were the result of greater forces beyond my control. All of the training in the world and all of the planning in the world could not change the fact that the weather was too hot and too humid. I may well continue to second guess myself, but I can rest assured that however much I do, at an age when most people are content to rest on their couches, I rode in blistering temperatures connected to dramatic changes in the weather that would have been even more devastating without my extensive training and careful planning.

Chapter 17
Cycles of Life

Cycles of Life is a travelogue, memoir, and history. As a travelogue it traces two bike "tours" from Brooklyn to Montreal, one in 1968 and the other in 2018, outlining the route taken and describing some of the sights along the way. As a memoir, the book examines my journeys in both years, centered on two major transitions in life. When I was seventeen, the bike ride tested me both mentally and physically, and although I was unaware of it at the time, the trek helped to guide me into adulthood. I was more conscious of the role the ride would play in my life as a sixty-seven-year-old. I was not really interested in recapturing a great moment from my youth. Instead, I wanted to use the ride to assist me in the adjustment I knew I was facing as I entered a life of "leisure." I was hoping that by training and then taking the ride I would ease myself into retirement and, by writing this book, I could speak to my generation as it faced the same challenge of leaving the workaday world. The book also serves as a history, comparing the changes and continuities between the two years, emphasizing the distinctiveness of the past from the present, and exploring the interaction between larger transformations and personal experience.

The cycles of life traced in these pages have allowed me to see both change and continuity over the last half century. In 1968 the political world was in the middle of a massive reconfiguration. The Republican Party was about to abandon its more moderate identity, move to the right, and appeal to a new base: the white Southerner who resented the interference of the federal government in their state. Ultimately, the issue that most compelled this shift was civil rights. This change was not necessarily linear, but from the high point in time, it has stayed with us and is in part responsible for the election of Donald J. Trump to the presidency. In 1968 the Southern Republican was a rarity; today they are the norm. Likewise, rust was beginning to corrode the great industrial belt of the Northeast and Midwest. Both the loss of my father's factory job and Joe's attraction to the demagogue George Wallace attest to the beginning of this development. We see a legacy of this shift in the Trump vote in places like Pennsylvania, Michigan, and Wisconsin and the desperate way a third of the nation clings to their support of the president regardless of his lies.

The history highlighted in this book encompasses more than politics and includes important developments in culture. The youth rebellion of the sixties, even though it did not lead to the political revolution many young people expected, spawned a series of social and cultural revolutions that have tentacles reaching to the present. The sexual revolution transformed the personal behavior of millions of Americans by 1968. It has continued unabated, leading in part to the greater acceptance of the LGBTQ community and has reshaped the family. The drug revolution has had less positive affects. By glorifying drug use, young people in the sixties opened the door to a pandora's box. The demons unleashed have their greatest impact today in the opioid epidemic that has devastated both rural and urban America. Another facet of the youth rebellion of the sixties was the casual revolution – a growing acceptance of less formal sartorial expression perhaps best represented in the years after 1968 in the emerging prominence of the tee shirt. Another aspect of this casual revolution was the growing acceptance of women wearing pants, epitomized by the pantsuits of Hillary Clinton and those donned by American women as part of the Pantsuit Nation on election day in 2016.

Of the many material objects that have altered our lives over the last fifty years, perhaps none has been more dramatic than the mechanisms we use to communicate. It is hard to imagine that the iPhone is only a little more than a decade old. Its ability to tap into social media, provide and record news has completely changed the way we relate to the outside world. More than simply the introduction of immediate television news in the 1960s and 1970s, the development of the personal computer in the 1980s, and even the emergence of the internet in the 1990s, the handheld device provides instantaneous information and is an item that we can always carry with us. College students consider it a "right" to have access to their personal electronics at all times, although as a scholar of the American Revolution I can assure the reader that there is nothing in the Bill of Rights about the "right to bear iPhones." The immediacy of these machines is astounding. On the 1968 ride, the only way we could connect with our families was by using a phone booth. And, because long-distance phone calls were expensive, we did so only once a day and always called collect. On the 2018 ride, we sent and received texts all day, our wives, and our family and friends could track our progress constantly. Our phones also provided detailed maps and directions at a swish of the finger. If we so desired, we could access news and almost any information we might desire.

The handheld device is an important reminder of how much has changed over the past fifty years and also how different the past is from the present. Superficial similarities obscure significant differences and violate the integrity of the past. In 1968, for instance, while many in the world admired American culture, they also decried the crass assertion of American power and the Vietnam War. American stock on the international scene, in other words, was at a low point. Today, once again American prestige is on the decline. This time the cause is not from an exertion of power in an unpopular war. Rather it is from the inconsistent policy and absurd assertions of the current president. Indeed, when Donald Trump proclaimed before the United Nations that he had achieved more in two years than any previous administration, the assembled delegates broke out into laughter. Making "America great again" has had little impact beyond the confines of the border that Trump wants to protect with a wall. History does not repeat itself. Instead every moment in the past is unique and has its own causes and explanations even as it is tied to everything that came before and everything that has occurred since.

As a historian, I am particularly aware of the interaction between the personal and the political. In fact, much of my published work has focused on the relationship between the two. I began my career by studying riots in early America and exploring the world of common sailors. This work gradually grew to include an examination of the interaction between those further down on the social scale with what in my academic youth I derisively called the "big shots" in history. This interest on how larger historical events affected regular people easily transfers to the story on these pages. Whatever my daily focus on the bike ride in 1968, I understood that when Joe, who graciously housed us in his home near Schenectady, ranted about the positive attributes of George Wallace, larger political forces were at work. When the border agents asked us if we were going into Canada to evade the draft, they were addressing a serious issue that could very well have an impact on my life.

When I was seventeen, I was just awakening into political consciousness. Nineteen sixty eight was a transitional year for me as I shifted to the left. That spring I was attracted to Robert Kennedy before he was eliminated by an assassin's bullet. After that tragic event, I had no one I wanted to support. In early November, I decided to go to the great pre-election Nixon rally held at Madison Square Garden with the idea that it would be interesting to see one of the two men who might become president. Joining me on the trip into "the city" – if you grew up in one of the outer boroughs, Manhattan was always referred to as "the city" – was Roger, and a few other friends. As we wended our way up the steps into the rally, with tickets in hand, the Nixon political machine swung into action. His security people were stationed every ten feet or so, attempting to weed out of the crowd any would-be demonstrators. I had marginally long hair and I had never really shaved so there were a few strands of blond peach fuzz sticking out from my chin. You could only see the facial hair if I tilted my head with a light behind my profile. Roger and the others had a similar appearance. Regardless, we were exactly what Nixon's "people" were looking for. One of these operatives grabbed my ticket and told me it was no good and that I should go home. Everyone else in my group somehow managed to get in. Roger, who was always quick thinking, had told the agent who tried to stop him that his father was just a few feet away. I was less creative. I figured that the crowd was so large that if I tried to enter a hundred feet further down the line and used my spare ticket, I should be able to get in. The wily Nixonite who had grabbed my first ticket would have none of it. Eyeing me from a distance, he shouted to another operative "Stop him, stop him, I have seen him before and he is trouble maker." Suddenly, I was surrounded by three or four young men in suits and my second ticket was gone. I gave up at that point and went home on the subway by myself convinced that "Tricky Dicky" was not my man.

Within a few years, as I headed to college and watched demonstration after demonstration break out on campuses across the United States, I became more radicalized. Safe from the draft with my student deferment, and then fortunate to have a "264" draft number when Nixon established a lottery for the selective service based on one's birth date, I came to realize the unfairness of a military system that guaranteed that if someone were poor and uneducated he (only young men were drafted) would be forced to serve in the military. I also recognized the futility of an interminable and unpopular war. Today pundits and politicians decry the bitterness of the chasm that separates Democrats and Republicans. As awful as these circumstances may appear, we seem to have forgotten what truly divisive politics looks like. By the late sixties many young people not only rejected the world of their parents, they embraced a counter culture that threatened to rend the nation asunder. A bombing campaign against institutions connected to the war effort began that only intensified in 1969 and 1970. In the spring of 1970, after the shootings at Kent State, and as I grew a beard and my hair reached to my shoulders, I became convinced that the nation was on the verge of a civil war.

Fifty years later I am one of those liberal professors decried by Trump and others. I deplore a Republican Party which has manipulated the political system to control the federal government despite obtaining fewer votes nationally in both presidential and congressional elections. I oppose a conservative agenda that denies the right of women to control their own bodies, ensures continued racial injustice, and favors the rich and corporations with tax breaks, while somehow convincing the uneducated that they support the little guy. I can also recognize the humanity and goodness of people with whom I disagree. David and I stand far apart on some issues and agree on others. For him abortion is murder, plain and simple. He also wants to see a more fiscally responsible approach to government. Yet he believes in equality, the need to preserve the environment, and the importance of having good and just people in government. We have discussed and debated these issues as we ran together for over twenty-five years. Whatever our differences, we enjoy each other's company and could easily join in the experience described in these pages.

In 2018 I was much more politically aware. Each day our hotel provided free copies of *USA Today* and, of course, we could watch both local and national news each morning and evening. Our iPhones sent us daily updates on what was happening beyond our immediate endeavor. Included in the information at our fingertips that week was the report of two deaths that can be seen as connecting the half century between 1968 and 2018: the passings of John McCain and Aretha Franklin. McCain was an American hero, whatever the president might think, who had been shot down by the North Vietnamese late in 1967. Although I did not know it at the time, when I was riding my bike in the summer of 1968, McCain was a prisoner of war, undergoing torture and abuse. A proponent of the war even after his return to the United States in 1973, he became a Republican senator from Arizona and a presidential candidate. Known for his ability to work across the aisle, he retained an independent streak to the very end. Franklin was an African American entertainer who supported the Civil Rights Movement. Her music ran the spectrum from gospel to jazz and the blues. In 1968 her image appeared on the cover of Time and her "R-E-S-P-E-C-T" spoke both to her gender and her race. By the end of the 1960s Franklin had become known as the "Queen of Soul." She remained an active performer the rest of her life. Her "Natural Woman," despite the fact that it centers on the attention of a man, has become emblematic of the women's movement. Together, the death of these two individuals reflect the passing of an age.

I also lost a close friend and colleague that week. She was one of the smartest and most articulate historians I knew. I was thunderstruck by the news since I did not even know that she was ill. As I sat in my hotel room at night recovering from the day's exertions, I found it all but impossible to respond to the messages I received concerning her death. Sixty seems to be a threshold when this type of news moves from a rarity to an all too frequent occurrence. I thought about this while I was on my ride. Even as I struggled with the four "Hs" from Hell, even as I made concessions to reality and cut out miles from the trip, I wondered why I had been so lucky. At age sixty-seven I could ride my bike hundreds of miles, while others my age faced illness and death. The capriciousness of life remains unfathomable.

Looking back to 1968 I now understand that my ride represented a major transition in my life. There was no single moment, no great rite of passage. Yet, by undertaking the bike ride, by venturing forth with Roger and Denis, I was marking my own independence and my shift from child to adult. It also provided me with a great story. For decades, I could refer to that ride and retell episodes from that adventure. I consciously embraced the 2018 ride with David as another major transition in my life. Again, there was no single moment, no great rite of passage. Yet, by seizing the opportunity to repeat the odyssey, just as I was moving from the life of a tenured professor to the life of a retiree, I was marking another shift in the great cycle of life. I now have new stories, many recorded here, to tell and retell. In 1968 I had a lifetime of great adventures in front of me. In 2018 I fully recognize my own mortality. I know that my strength has already begun to ebb from me and that I will only weaken further. Death awaits us all. The ride reminded me of that. It also reminded me that I still have a lifetime of adventures to come.

About the Author

Paul A. Gilje was born in Brooklyn in 1951, attended New York City public schools before going to Brooklyn College where he earned a BA in history. He grew up in a working-class immigrant household: in 1936, at age seventeen, his father arrived in the United States from Norway and his mother was born to Polish parents in Williamsburg, Brooklyn. After college he attended Brown University, earning his PhD in 1980.

Upon graduation, he moved to Norman, Oklahoma to take a position at the University of Oklahoma. There he worked his way through the academic ranks and in 2008 was awarded the highest research distinction offered by the university – he became a George Lynn Cross Research Professor. His history writing focuses on the American Revolution and the early republic. He began his career as a social historian, but after 2000 he increasingly sought to integrate social, political and cultural history in his publications, including, *Liberty on the Waterfront: American Maritime Society and Culture in the Age of Revolution, 1750-1850* (2004), which won two national prizes, including the "best book" award from the Society for Historians of the Early American Republic and more recently *Free Trade and Sailors' Rights in the War of 1812* (2013) and *To Swear Like a Sailor: Maritime Culture in America, 1750-1850* (2016). Gilje has written two books on the history of rioting in the United States and a synthetic examination of the revolutionary and early republic eras. In addition, he has edited five essay collections, and has published two encyclopedia projects, including the three-volume *Encyclopedia of Revolutionary America*. He has presented his research at conferences throughout the United States and in

Europe and has received numerous grants and fellowships to support his research. Gilje was an award-winning teacher who offered a wide variety of courses at both the undergraduate and graduate levels before retiring on December 31, 2017. In 2009-10, he served as president of the Society for Historians of the Early American Republic. Currently he is working on a book on the year 1800, which will provide a political narrative of the climatic events of the election of that year interspersed with vignettes of everyday life for common people.

In 1973 he married Ann. Together they raised two children, Erik and Karin who went on to earn doctorates themselves – but not in history. Ann and Paul enjoy traveling, love spending time with their expanding brood of grandchildren, and currently reside in Philadelphia, Pennsylvania. Even after his 2018 cycling journey, Paul and Ann still go riding on their bicycles. Indeed, on any given morning, you are likely to see Paul out on Schuylkill River Trail either jogging (now at a twelve-minute-a-mile pace) or proudly riding his Trek FXS-5.